NINE GATES

▼ ▼ ▼ ▼ ▼ ▼ ▼ ▼ ▼ ▼ ▼ ▼ ▼ ▼ ▼ ▼ ▼ ▼

Books by Jane Hirshfield

POETRY
The Lives of the Heart
The October Palace
Of Gravity & Angels
Alaya

ESSAYS
Nine Gates: Entering the Mind of Poetry

ANTHOLOGY
Women in Praise of the Sacred: 43 Centuries
  of Spiritual Poetry by Women

TRANSLATION (*with Mariko Aratani*)
The Ink Dark Moon: Love Poems by Ono no
  Komachi and Izumi Shikibu, Women of
  the Ancient Court of Japan

NINE GATES

Entering the Mind of Poetry

▼ ▼ ▼ ▼ ▼ ▼ ▼ ▼ ▼ ▼ ▼

Essays by Jane Hirshfield

HarperCollins*Publishers*

NINE GATES: ENTERING THE MIND OF POETRY. Copyright ©
1997 by Jane Hirshfield. All rights reserved. Printed in the United
States of America. No part of this book may be used or reproduced
in any manner whatsoever without written permission except in
the case of brief quotations embodied in critical articles and
reviews. For information address HarperCollins Publishers, Inc.,
10 East 53rd Street, New York, NY 10022.

HarperCollins books may be purchased for educational, business,
or sales promotional use. For information please write: Special
Markets Department, HarperCollins Publishers, Inc., 10 East 53rd
Street, New York, NY 10022.

FIRST EDITION

Designed and typeset by David Bullen

Library of Congress Cataloging-in-Publication Data
Hirshfield, Jane, 1953–
    Nine gates : entering the mind of poetry / by Jane Hirshfield.
       p.   cm.
    ISBN 0–06–017456–0
    1. Poetics. 2. Poetry—History and Criticism. I. Title.
    PN1042.H49   1997
    808.1—dc21   97–2793

97 98 99 00 01 ❖/RRD 10 9 8 7 6 5 4 3 2

Contents

▼　　▼　　▼　　▼　　▼　　▼　　▼　　▼　　▼　　▼

Preface

▼　　▼　　▼　　▼　　▼　　▼　　▼　　▼　　▼

Poetry's work is the clarification and magnification of being. Each time we enter its word-woven and musical invocation, we give ourselves over to a different mode of knowing: to poetry's knowing, and to the increase of existence it brings, unlike any other. This book is an attempt to understand more fully that particular mode of comprehension. It is an exploration of some of the pathways words take toward meaning, and an effort to investigate poetry's gestures and conduct, to map a part of the terrain where it lives.

To think consciously about the distinctive forms of poetry's perceptive speech isn't necessary before participating in the activity and grace of poetic mind—that mind and its music come first. Still, in trying to understand the ways a poem may carry itself into comprehension and beauty, I have always found an added resonance and pleasure. Here, as elsewhere in life, attentiveness only deepens what it regards. Yet I hope that present in this book are not only ideas about the art of poetry and its workings, but also some part of my gratitude, respect, and wonder at the mysterious informing it offers to all who pass through its gate.

These pieces were first written over a ten-year period, presented at various occasions when people gathered to talk about poems and literature and the pursuit of good writing. Because each began as a free-standing piece, certain themes and quotations recur; in several cases, a thought that arose while writing one essay became the central idea explored in another. Removing repetition entirely has proved impossible, but I hope readers will forgive this book's occasionally overlapping concerns.

Initial versions of most of these pieces have appeared, in whole or in part, in a number of periodicals, which I here thank: *The American Poetry Review, The Associated Writing Programs Chronicle, The Georgia Review, The New England Review, Poetry Flash,* and *The Seattle Review.* A shorter version of "Facing the Lion" also appeared in the book *Facing The Lion: Best Talks From Writers' Conferences and Festivals,* volume 2 (Boston: Beacon Press, 1996).

I am grateful as well to those whose requests to speak about poetry occasioned these ideas: The Napa Valley Writers Conference, The Port Townsend Writers Conference, The University of Alaska at Fairbanks, The Portland Poetry Symposium, The Art of the Wild Writers Conference, The Haiku Society of North America, Naropa College's M.F.A. Program in Poetics, The Truckee Meadows Writers Conference, The Alan Watts Society and the California Institute of Integral Studies, and Bennington College's M.F.A. Writing Seminars.

During the time I worked on these pieces I also received generous support for my work from a number of institutions. I thank The John Simon Guggenheim Memorial Foundation, The Rockefeller Foundation's Bellagio Study and Conference Center, Yaddo, The MacDowell

Colony, and The Djerassi Resident Artists Program for their assistance and hospitality.

I thank also the friends in poetry who have talked with me about these pieces over the years, most notably Laura Fargas, Dorianne Laux, and Kay Ryan. Lewis Hyde's thoughts on Trickster in the mind of art have been fertile sources in a number of ways. Over the past year of rewriting the essays, many virtually completely, Katy Butler's editorial and human insight has been invaluable in every way. And finally, I thank Michael Katz, Hugh van Dusen, Jisho Cary Warner, and David Bullen; without each of them, the book you hold in your hands would not exist.

NINE GATES

Entering the Mind of Poetry

▼   ▼   ▼   ▼   ▼   ▼   ▼   ▼   ▼   ▼   ▼

A note about the translations: Any translations not otherwise credited were made by the author, except for all translations of poems by Izumi Shikibu or Ono no Komachi, which were made by the author in collaboration with Mariko Aratani.

Poetry and the Mind of Concentration

▾ ▾   ▾   ▾   ▾   ▾   ▾   ▾   ▾   ▾

Every good poem begins in language awake to its own connections—language that hears itself and what is around it, sees itself and what is around it, looks back at those who look into its gaze and knows more perhaps even than we do about who and what we are. It begins, that is, in the body and mind of concentration.

By concentration, I mean a particular state of awareness: penetrating, unified, and focused, yet also permeable and open. This quality of consciousness, though not easily put into words, is instantly recognizable. Aldous Huxley described it as the moment the doors of perception open; James Joyce called it epiphany. The experience of concentration may be quietly physical—a simple, unexpected sense of deep accord between yourself and everything. It may come as the harvest of long looking and leave us, as it did Wordsworth, amid thought "too deep for tears." Within action, it is felt as a grace state: time slows and extends, and a person's every movement and decision seem to partake of perfection. Concentration can be also placed into things—it radiates undimmed from Vermeer's paintings, from the small marble figure of a lyre-player from prehistoric Greece, from a Chinese three-footed bowl—and into musical notes, words, ideas. In the whole-heartedness of concentration, world and self begin to cohere. With that state comes an enlarging: of what may be known, what may be felt, what may be done.

A request for concentration isn't always answered, but people engaged in many disciplines have found ways to invite it in. A ninth-century Zen monk, Zuigan, could be heard talking to himself rather sternly each morning: "Master Zuigan!" he would call out. "Yes?" "Are you here?" "Yes!" Violinists practicing scales and dancers repeating the same movements over decades are not simply warming up or mechanically training their muscles. They are learning how to attend unswervingly, moment by moment, to themselves and their art; learning to come into steady presence, free from the distractions of interest or boredom.

Writers, too, must find a path into concentration. Some keep a fixed time of day for writing, or engage in small rituals of preparation and invitation. One may lay out exactly six freshly sharpened pencils, another may darken the room, a third may develop as odd a routine as Flaubert, who began each workday by sniffing a drawer of aging apples. Immersion in art itself can be the place of entry, as Adam Zagajewski points out in "A River": "Poems from poems, songs / from songs, paintings from paintings." Yet however it is brought into being, true concentration appears—paradoxically—at the moment willed effort drops away. It is then that a person enters what scientist Mihaly Csikszentmihalyi has described as "flow" and Zen calls "effortless effort." At such moments, there may be some strong emotion present—a feeling of joy, or even grief—but as often, in deep concentration, the self disappears. We seem to fall utterly into the object of our attention, or else vanish into attentiveness itself.

This may explain why the creative is so often described as impersonal and beyond self, as if inspiration were literally what its etymology implies, something "breathed in." We refer, however metaphorically, to the Muse, and speak of profound artistic discovery as revelation. And however much we may come to believe that "the real" is subjective and constructed, we still feel art is a path not just to beauty, but to truth: if "truth" is a chosen narrative, then new stories, new aesthetics, are also new truths.

Difficulty itself may be a path toward concentration—expended effort weaves us into a task, and successful engagement, however laborious, becomes also a labor of love. The work of writing brings replenishment even to the writer dealing with painful subjects or working out formal problems, and there are times when suffering's only open path is through an immersion in what is. The eighteenth-century Urdu poet Ghalib described the principle this way: "For the raindrop, joy is in entering the river—/ Unbearable pain becomes its own cure."

Difficulty then, whether of life or of craft, is not a hindrance to an artist. Sartre called genius "not a gift, but the way a person invents in desperate circumstances." Just as geological pressure transforms ocean sediment to limestone, the pressure of an artist's concentration goes into the making of any fully realized work. Much of beauty, both in art and in life, is a balancing of the lines of forward-flowing desire with those of resistance—a gnarled tree, the flow of a statue's draped cloth. Through such tensions, physical or mental, the world in which we exist becomes itself. Great art, we might say, is thought that has been concentrated in just this way: honed and shaped by a silky attention brought to bear on the recalcitrant matter of earth and of life. We seek in art the elusive intensity by which it knows.

▾ ▾ ▾

CONCENTRATION's essence is kinetic, and the dictionary shows the verb as moving in three directions. The first definition of "to concentrate" is *to direct toward a common center*. This form of concentration pulls a poem together, making of its disparate parts a single event. A lyric poem can be seen as a number of words that, taken as a whole, become a new, compound word, whose only possible definition is the poem itself. That unity of purpose is a poem's integrity and oneness, drawing it inward and toward coherence.

The second definition is *to focus one's attention;* this aspect of concentration faces outward, and has to do with the feeling of clarity a good poem brings to both writer and reader. Clarity does not mean simplicity, or even ease of understanding—at times, only the most complex rendering can do justice to an experience, and other times, ambiguity itself is a poem's goal. Still, one of Ezra Pound's definitions of poetry was "the best words in the best order." Walt Whitman wrote, "The fruition of beauty is no chance of hit or miss. . . . It is inevitable as life . . . exact and plumb as gravitation." This second kind of concentration moves then into exactitude, a precise connecting. Focusing on its object, it rinses clean and grounds both poem and world.

The third definition is *to increase in strength or density*, as in concentrating a salt solution. The direction of movement here is in another dimension entirely, neither inward nor outward: it is our own state of being that alters. Concentration of this kind relates to the way a poem's presentation of meaning opposes not chaos—which is just a stage of transformation—but the laziness and entropy of ordinary mind.

This intensification is one reason certain words persist at the center of our lives. Through poetry's concentration great sweeps of thought, emotion, and perception are compressed to forms the mind is able to hold—into images, sentences, and stories that serve as entrance tokens to large and often slippery realms of being. Consider William Butler Yeats's "The Second Coming"—its "rough beast, slouching toward Bethlehem," or, from the same poem, the lines, "The best lack all conviction, while the worst / Are full of passionate intensity." Whether image or abstract statement, these words hold fast in the mind, seeded with the surplus of beauty and meaning that is concentration's mark.

Finally, concentration is one translation of *dhyana*, the Sanskrit term—source of the Chinese *chan* and Japanese *zen*—that describes the one-pointed mind of meditation. In the Western word's etymology, we find a related concept, *kentron*: the Greek word for the sharp point at the center, from a verb meaning "to prick." When you go to concentration's center, you are pricked, which should mean you wake up—exactly what a good poem helps you do.

▼   ▼   ▼   ▼   ▼

THE forms concentration can take when placed into the words of poems are probably infinite. Still, six emerge as central energies through which poetry moves forward into the world it creates— the concentrations of music, rhetoric, image, emotion, story, and voice. Not all work at the same level, and in any particular poem each will always coexist with at least some of the others; yet each can at times stand at the core of a poem's speaking.

POETRY has historically been defined as particular ways of organizing thought through sound, and its music remains the point where any good poem begins. We take our first, sheer joy in audible language before birth, as we listen from within the womb to the particular murmur of life in a human community and body. Heard speech remains a doorway and invitation throughout our lives, and every poem, whether traditional or free verse, must feel alive and grounded in its speaking before it will live in any other way.

The musical qualities of verse create their own concentration. Prosody draws the mind into a heightened alertness in which other powers of insight and imagination may also come into being; its forms bring a poem together, urging the memorable compression in which poetry begins. But a poem's interweavings of sound do something else as well: they signal the way every part of a poem affirms its connection with all the rest, each element speaking to and with every other. A glittering, multifaceted expression of interconnection is among poetry's central gifts.

One way poetry connects is across time. Saying a poem aloud, or reading it silently if we do so with our full attention, our bodies as well as our minds enter the rhythms present at that poem's conception. We breathe as the author breathed, we move our own tongue and teeth and throat in the ways they moved in the poem's first making. There is a startling intimacy to this. Some echo of a writer's physical experience comes into us when we read her poem; if the poem is our own, it is our own past that reinhabits our bodies, at least in part. Shaped language is strangely immortal, living in a meadowy freshness outside of time.

But it also lives in the moment, in us. Emotion, intellect, and physiology are inseparably connected in the links of a poem's sound. It is difficult to feel intimacy while shouting, to rage in a low whisper, to skip and weep at the same time. The cadences and music a poem makes within us join to create its feeling-tone as well. The difference between irony and sincerity, for instance, is conveyed by subtle verbal cues, small shifts of pitch and rhythm. A good measure of content can live in such distinctive patterns of sound.

The repetition and changes of a poem's prosody are the outward face of inner transformation. Unfolding their tensions and resolutions, a poem's sounds make of experience a shapeliness, with beginning, middle, and end. And under every poem's music, whether in form or free verse, lies the foundational heartbeat, its drum and assurance accompanying us through our lives. One of prosody's promises, then, is of a continuing, coherent existence. Some readers object to formal verse for just this reason. They feel in it a worldview too orderly for the chaos and uncertainty of contemporary life. Yet to write in a traditional form is to find that a regular returning in one dimension can bring unexpected turns in another: hunting a rhyme, the mind falls on a wholly surprising idea. This balancing between expected and unforeseen, both in aesthetic and cognitive structures, is near the center of every work of art. Through the gate of concentration, defining yet open, both aspects enter.

A POEM's music affects us whether or not we make it conscious; still, to study sound's workings reawakens both ear and poem. Generalization cannot teach this alertness. It is learned only by saying one poem at a time aloud, completely. Voicing it repeatedly, feeling its weights and measures, sounding its vowels; noticing where in the body each syllable comes to rest; tasting the consonants' motion through lips and tongue. Then saying it yet again, this time hearing the meaning, and hearing how music and content not only support one another but are indistinguishably one. A good choice is Yeats's "The Lake Isle of Innisfree." A work that sounds like water over rocks or wind in trees, it holds not only the music of human thought and feeling but also the music of earth in its words.

The Lake Isle of Innisfree

I will arise and go now, and go to Innisfree,
And a small cabin build there, of clay and wattles made:
Nine bean rows will I have there, a hive for the honeybee,
And live alone in the bee-loud glade.

And I shall have some peace there, for peace comes dropping slow,
Dropping from the veils of the morning to where the cricket sings;
There midnight's all a glimmer, and noon a purple glow,
And evening full of the linnet's wings.

I will arise and go now, for always night and day
I hear lake water lapping with low sounds by the shore;
While I stand on the roadway, or on the pavements grey,
I hear it in the deep heart's core.

This poem's form is traditional; still, as with any good poem, its musical strength lies in its subtler workings. The regular rhyme scheme plays against large variations of meter; stresses and rhythms continually shift. Iambs move into spondees, lines with caesuras' internal pauses turn into lines that flow unobstructed to their end. And most powerfully, the changing vowels and consonants carry music's literal informing: *s*s and *l* sounds bind the poem together while the light vowels of "glimmer" and "linnet" give way to the long *a*s and *o*s of the final stanza.

Any few sentences can scarcely describe how Yeats's prosody weaves a world; readers must finish the exercise for themselves. Yet even on a first hearing, by the time "I hear lake water lapping with low sounds by the shore" arrives, it is the lake itself to which we listen. Then comes the slow and slowing rhythm of "deep heart's core." Those three strong beats, holding the long *e* that is the poem's bass note, bring us to the close of the poem far within our own being, plunged into the longing for such a place, where only the essential asks our attention. It is a place of solitude's beauty and silence, of thought beyond words—that words' music has made.

▼   ▼   ▼   ▼   ▼

Before we can concentrate easily, we need to know where we stand. This is the work of rhetoric, to locate words and reader in time and place, in situation and point of view. Sound invites concentration by engaging the body and the emotions; rhetoric draws in and focuses the cognitive mind. Traditionally defined as the art of choosing the words that will best convey the speaker's intent, rhetoric's concern is the precise and beautiful movement of mind in language.

Americans distrust artful speech, believing that sincerity and deliberation cannot coexist. The sentiment has roots in the last century: "A line will take us hours, maybe; / Yet if it does not seem a moment's thought, / Our stitching and unstitching has been naught," Yeats wrote in "Adam's Curse." Romantic temperament, he knew, equates spontaneity and truth. But the word *art* is neighbor to *artifice,* and in human culture, as in the animal and vegetable worlds, desirability entails not only the impulse of the moment but also enhancement, exaggeration, rearrangement, and deception. We don't find the fragrance of night-scented flowering tobacco or the display of a peacock's tail insincere—by such ruses this world conducts its erotic business. To acknowledge rhetoric's presence in the beauty of poems, or any other form of speech, is only to agree to what already is.

Rhetoric persuades at a level so immediate it is scarcely conscious, and spelling out its workings can often seem tedious: the mind moves more quickly than that. Yet this potent, subliminal grounding is nonetheless chosen and worth exploring, and so the first tool lifted in rhetoric's shop is a basic question: "Who is speaking to whom, and toward what end?" The question's simplicity is deceptive: in its answering, many shadow devices of meaning-making step into light.

In poetry, though, one element precedes even this: that a poem is a poem is itself essential rhetorical information. The organization of white space and ink or the vocal tones that signal "poetry" are instructions to reader or listener to enter the changed consciousness that poetry asks. Each element of a poem is expected to be meaningful, part of a shaped and shaping experience of a whole: a word's placement on the page is significant, not accidental; sound qualities matter; even punctuation is thoroughly alive, responsive to itself and its context. To feel how, reading poetry, we shift instinctively into these altered expectations and assumptions, consider "found" poems. Just as Duchamp's urinal changed in nature when placed in a gallery setting, a newspaper article or recipe placed into poetry's lines is recast: the new form signals us, in reading it, to listen for concentration's transforming arc.

THE power of "The Lake Isle of Innisfree" lies in its marriage of music and meaning, and rhetoric too plays its role in our encounter with that poem. First comes the visual (or auditory) recognition that what we are entering is a poem. Next, we absorb the title's message that these words concern a place, and immediately we wait to see how that place will be filled—in poetry, a landscape is never only outer, it is also a portrait of a state of soul. With the text's first word, we discover the poem is in the first person; with the second, we find the speaker making a statement about the future. Already, we are intuiting what kind of "I" this may be, probably guessing it is the poet speaking directly. (The other possibility is a more fictional "I," familiar from first-person novels or from dramatic monologues such as Robert Browning's "My Last Duchess.")

While forming a hypothesis about the speaker, we listen at the same time for some idea of whom the "I" may address. Two possibilities come to mind. One is that the poet speaks to a specific person, present in the poet's mind if not on the page. In some poems, this implied listener turns out to be the reader himself. But here it seems most likely the poem is a private meditation, spoken by the self to the self and "overheard" by the reader. This second interpretation, though odd when described in the abstract, is the rhetoric of many first-person lyric poems—since before the advent of literacy, poetry has served as a vessel in which solitary thought might occur.

As the reader makes his way through a poem, these initial hypotheses are tested and either confirmed or revised. Also continually held in the mind is the third part of rhetoric's basic question: Why am I being told these things? What will I know by the end of this poem I did not know before? For in the realm of poetry, the answer to the question, Toward what end? is almost always twofold: an ostensible speaker and listener and reason for speaking appear within the context of the poem, but another dialogue also takes place, between writer and reader. Here, the *who* is the poet, the *whom* is the reader, and the *end* is the experience we take from the poem, the reason for speech rather than silence. (Occasionally, the two rhetorical frames may meet, as they do when the reader of a love poem is the beloved to whom it is addressed, or when the author of a private meditative lyric reads her own work.)

Every reading reflects not only the poem but also the reader, and so answers to the third part of rhetoric's question will differ. For me, "The Lake Isle of Innisfree" haunts first with the image of a life stripped down to the grace of essentials; it speaks of the sustenance and mystery of the simple; of the chance that, by paying attention to only what matters, one may find the heart's deep hungers and daily existence joined together and made whole. But good poems always hold more than one knowledge, and Yeats's words speak as well the impossibility of such a life. The poet proclaims his departure, yet the last stanza finds him standing undeparted, amid Dublin's streets: he listens to the siren call while remaining in place, as he has, night and day, for some time. The island of Innisfree is irresistible and unobtainable, a dream simultaneously praised and mourned. It is a figure, perhaps, for the fate of everything we desire and cannot have. This unease about the poem's outcome tugs half-recognized beneath its sureness of surface. That undertow is no small part of how a seemingly simple poem carries in the end so mysteriously powerful an effect.

RHETORIC's various devices make a vast contribution to a poem's meaning, power, and grace. For instance, if a poem's basic grammatical strategy is changed, its meaning will shift as well. Imagine the first line of Yeats's poem to read "You must arise and go now," or "Yesterday I arose and went"—either would lead to an entirely different work.

Similarly important is the order in which a poem's elements arrive: order shapes not only the rhythms of a poem's unfolding, but also its statement. When William Carlos Williams writes of the importance of the common by describing a red wheelbarrow "glazed with rain / water // beside the white / chickens," it makes a difference that the chickens, those unpoetic creatures, are what we meet last—if its endnote were the more "poetic" image of rain, rather than chickens, the poet's meaning would be undercut. Similarly Williams's many line breaks work to slow the mind, to focus the attention on a brief poem; the placement of free verse on the page has rhetorical as well as musical meaning.

Apparently minor grammatical choices can have large rhetorical effects—the choice of a pronoun, for example, or of the definite or indefinite article. Again, a small experiment makes it clear: compare "Outside my window, I saw the bird" with "Outside the window, I saw a bird." In the first sentence, we are in a place the speaker considers home, seeing a bird with which there is or will be a particular relationship; in the second, none of this is true. And while we might assume the more particularizing grammar will always be "better," some statements require exactly the second, general grammatical strategy. When Emily Dickinson begins, "A bird came down the walk," we know immediately what is familiar to her, what new; that author and bird are strangers makes a difference, for both the opening and the end of her poem.

Beginnings are useful places to feel how rhetoric engages the cognitive mind. As soon as we've heard Shakespeare's "Shall I compare thee to a summer's day?" we lean to hear how the rest of the sonnet will fulfill the comparison. A strong opening proposition is another way to snare the attention, as in W. H. Auden's "Musée des Beaux Arts": "About suffering they were never wrong, / The Old Masters . . ." We can be called to wakefulness by a puzzle, as in Czeslaw Milosz's statements: "Rivers grow small. Cities grow small. And splendid gardens / show what we did not see there before: crippled leaves and dust." By their interest or strangeness, such openings raise a question, an anticipation in the mind. How does a river or city grow small? What is it the Old Masters knew about suffering? These unanswered questions carry the reader forward, alert and curious, into the poem. Even so small a gesture as opening a poem with a prepositional phrase ("In the garden" or "At dawn") has its effect—the reader enters the poem both grounded in physical being and in motion, situated in time or place and looking for what comes next.

Finally, there are poems whose rhetoric consists of an undisguised manipulation of grammar. Gwendolyn Brooks, in "A Lovely Love," rings sorrowful, imperative stage directions directly into the reader's ear: "Let it be alleys. Let it be a hall / Whose janitor javelins epithets and thought / To cheapen hyacinth darkness. . ." This is a poet creating reality by force of will. Philip Levine, too, characteristically moves his poems by deliberate changes of grammar. His poem "What Work Is," for example, alternates between the second-person "you," in which the speaker addresses the reader, and the "you" that is a colloquial substitute for "I." When at the poem's close they become one, the synthesis is no small part of the poem's power, though it is doubtful readers will have spelled out for themselves just what has occurred.

To be aware of a poem's effects—aware of the expectations raised by each new word and aware of how the poem satisfies and changes those expectations throughout its course—does not require naming every moment's strategic gesture. It requires only our alert responsiveness, our presence to each shift in the currents of language with an answering shift in our own being. Poems, despite the ways they are sometimes taught, are not crossword-puzzle constructions; first drafts, and many stages of revision, take place at a level closer to daydream. But daydream with an added intensity: while writing, the mind moves between consciousness and the unconscious in the effortless effort of concentration. The result, if the poet's intensity of attention is sufficient, will be a poem that brims with its own knowledge, water trembling as if miraculously above the edge of a cup. Such a poem will be perfect in the root sense of the word: "thoroughly done."

In the concentration of poetry, rhetoric not only reflects intention but shapes it: the clarity of the writer and the clarities of syntax, word choice, and grammar are not one-directional, but two. Making a poem is neither a wholly conscious activity nor an act of unconscious transcription—it is a way for new thinking and feeling to come into existence, a way in which disparate modes of meaning and being may join. This is why the process of revising a poem is no arbitrary tinkering, but a continued honing of the self at the deepest level. Yeats describes revision's work in an untitled quatrain, epigraph to his 1908 *Collected Poems:*

The friends that have it I do wrong
when ever I remake a song,
Should know what issue is at stake:
it is myself that I remake.

▾   ▾   ▾   ▾   ▾

In *ABC of Reading,* Ezra Pound describes poetic meaning as taking three primary forms. First, he names melopoeia, a poem's music. Second, there is logopoeia, a poem's intellectual component. We come now to his third power: phanopoeia, the making of images.

Image's concentration, like sound's, is a field where the energies of mind and body meet. The deepest of image's meanings is its recognition of our continuity with the rest of existence: within a good image, outer and subjective worlds illumine one another, break bread together, converse. In this way, image increases both vision and what is seen. Keeping one foot braced in the physical and the other in the realm of inner experience, image enlivens both.

How does this interconnection of animate and inanimate, exterior and interior, work? Consider two images from Philip Larkin's "Here" (a portrait of the English city of Hull), each intermingling abstraction and felt life: "Here silence stands / like heat" and "Here is unfenced existence: / Facing the sun, untalkative, out of reach." Though the poem describes Hull's oppression and dullness, in each sentence the inanimate quickens, breathes. Silence, given a body through both synaesthesia and verb choice, takes on a muscular presence. Existence, even less sensory, is brought also into the world's woven fabric, first by being "unfenced" (the fence is there, splintery and palpable, even when placed into consciousness within the negative) and then by being situated, as silence has been, in familiar bodily life—"facing the sun" and "untalkative" are human attributes. Still, these images are no simplistic personification. They are forms that let us inhabit abstraction as if from within, and so begin to know our kinship with the wide field of being. They show the way poetry moves consciousness toward empathy.

Intelligence and receptivity are connected—human meaning is made by seeing into what is. Larkin's images show how the outer world can be transformed by a subjectively infused vision; inner event placed into the language of the physical takes on an equally mysterious addition. This comes in part from the way image summons the body into a poem. It comes as well from the surplus of perception a good image emits, like an extra light: in one set of words, more than one knowledge resides. "Evening full of the linnet's wings" is physical description. It is also Yeats's imagination of a possible state of inner life. Each reading enriches and magnifies the other.

Image-making, wrote Wallace Stevens, "is primarily a discipline of rightness." In a good image, something previously unformulated (in the most literal sense) comes into the realm of the expressed. Without precisely this image, we feel, the world's store of truth would be diminished; and conversely, when a writer brings into language a new image that is fully right, what is knowable of existence expands. A new image transforms, but its rightness is rooted in what already exists—the senses' witness. Image is taken up by the reaching mind, but also within the welcoming ears, the tongue's four recognitions, the muscles' familiar surge of kinship. "With my whole body I taste these peaches," wrote Stevens, and it is by our own bodies that we know what this means.

Thinking within the fields of image, the mind crosses also into the knowledge the unconscious holds—into the shape-shifting wisdom of dream. Poetic concentration allows us to bring the dream-mind's compression, displacement, wit, depth, and surprise into our waking minds. It is within dreamlife we first learn to read rain as grief, or the way that a turtle's walking may speak of containment and an awkward, impeccable fortitude. The need for such entrance to the unconscious may be why the story of Orpheus requires Eurydice's death—it brings the singer into the underworld journey necessary for poetry's work. Her loss causes as well the outpouring of longing and grief that companion our knowledge that beauty cannot be possessed; a longing and grief that, having nowhere else to go, become in Orpheus, as in Yeats, the source of song.

To INVESTIGATE the image at work, here are two poems; the first is an early poem of mourning, by Sharon Olds.

The Winter After Your Death

The long bands of mellow light
across the snow
narrow slowly.
The sun closes her gold fan
and nothing is left but black and white—
the quick steam of my breath, the dead
accurate shapes of the weeds, still, as if
pressed in an album.
Deep in my body my green heart
turns, and thinks of you. Deep in the
pond, under the thick trap
door of ice, the water moves,
the carp hangs like a sun, its scarlet
heart visible in its side.

The poem begins in the wholly literal world, but moves quickly into the imaginal with the appearance of the female sun. This person-ification, more conspicuous than Larkin's, risks pulling the poem into sentimentality; yet it does not, perhaps because the sun of the poem's closing image is so stark. In any case, this sun folding her gold fan is also a rather lovely and old-fashioned image, introducing the colors that carry the poem's emotion forward as they shift from gold to black and white, then into the startling green heart of the poet and the equally startling scarlet one of the carp.

The poem (whose fourteen lines, with a shift between the first eight and the last six, signal us that it is vestigially a sonnet) moves through four sentences, each more inward in nature. From simple and outward visual description, both grammar and imagery move into a realm more complex and more personal: the sun of the second sentence is feminine; the poet appears in the white steam of breath; the weeds, both directly and through their comparison with pressed flowers, speak of the death that goes otherwise unmentioned in the poem's body. The third sentence is again grammatically simple, yet its surreal green heart contains tremendous power. And as the heart turns, the poem turns, into the interior transparencies of the fourth sentence, where ice and water and carp are equal presences.

The images of "The Winter After Your Death" embody the twin depths, literal and figurative, of internal and external worlds. Everything pulls in two directions: the ice that is not only a trap door but also, because of the line break, a trap that is not a door; the visible heart of the fish that becomes not only life, but also—because what is ordinarily hidden within is now seen—the body's fragile mortality. The whole poem is a passage into the underworld made through the eyes, but one that returns us as well to the living. The displacement of loss into simile allows outer seeing to shift into the inner world, where what has vanished can still be known. Weeds pass from the actual into the realm of memory. The sun vanished from the beginning of the poem returns, transformed. That blood-red image offers only a vulnerable salvation, but it is one that must do.

IN "The Winter After Your Death," every detail is multiple in meaning, as with the images in dream; however actual it seems at the start, the landscape of the poem becomes metaphor, entirely the terrain of mourning. But the world of objects can appear in poems in plainer ways as well, staying close to how we live in ordinary relationship with things—to the way bedsheet, shoes, window, cup, and fork are our constant and given companions. Here, a shoe is a shoe. Yet these images too can open us into a wider understanding, as in "The Fishing-Tackle," written by Bertolt Brecht when he was a refugee in southern California during World War II. It is a poem that investigates the objective world as it is, rather than transformed to another purpose, and that is part of the point. Keeping faithful to primary life was Brecht's ethic as well as his aesthetic.

The Fishing-Tackle

In my room, on the whitewashed wall
Hangs a short bamboo stick bound with cord
With an iron hook designed
To snag fishing nets from the water. The stick
Came from a second-hand store downtown. My son
Gave it to me for my birthday. It is worn.
In salt water the hook's rust has eaten through the binding.
These traces of use and of work
Lend great dignity to the stick. I
Like to think that this fishing-tackle
Was left behind by those Japanese fishermen
Whom they have now driven from the West Coast into camps
As suspect aliens; that it came into my hands
To keep me in mind of so many
Unsolved but not insoluble
Questions of humanity.

(trans. Lee Baxendall)

Like "The Winter After Your Death," "The Fishing-Tackle" begins with straightforward description. We are given a room with a whitewashed wall, on which hangs what was once an implement of work and is now an ornament. The tool is described simply, but at some length: by the duration of his interest as much as by what he says, Brecht shows this object as worthy of attention. Its substance, the story of how it came to him, the way it is rusted and worn—more than half the poem stays rooted in this factual realm. Only then are we told the questions the tool's presence raises in the poet's mind, and only the most subtle hint, the phrase "that it came into my hands," signals us to remember Brecht's own relationship to the story. To remember, that is, a great deal: Brecht's position as a refugee from another country with which America is at war. Our knowledge that he too has been forced to abandon his primary work. The difference between the poet's own freedom and the previous owner's confinement in a camp. The question of what happens to a thing (or a person) forcibly removed from its living context. Brecht leaves the reader to name for herself these "unsolved but not insoluble questions," and this too is a sign of respect. The poet trusts we will choose to ponder with him the harsh koan of how we treat one another and why.

As "The Winter After Your Death" leaves much of its meaning unspoken, so, too, does the "The Fishing-Tackle." In each poem, the reader is given the data of image and only enough information to understand what terrain he is in, then left to complete the work himself: to furnish what has been left out with his own awareness, poetic concentration, and knowledge of inner and outer worlds. Olds has placed the background information into her title, while Brecht has put his into the body of the poem; but if we doubt that the concentration of image is as much the core of the latter poem as the former, we have only to try an experiment. First, give it the title "Considering the Japanese Fishermen Put into Camps," and cut the poem to its first seven lines. While the result is another work than the actual version, it remains a poem, both meaningful and moving. But try to read "The Fishing-Tackle" starting with "I like to think" and it oddly evaporates, all its power vanished. In this test we begin to feel the work image performs in poems.

▾   ▾   ▾   ▾   ▾

WHILE difficult to consider in isolation, passion is another fundamental energy in the making of poems. Strong emotion is concentrating by definition: overtaken by passion, we think of nothing else. Powerful feeling rushes language forward in distinctive and recognizable ways. Think of Christopher Smart's "Jubilate Agno," Allen Ginsberg's "Howl," Emily Dickinson's "Wild Nights, Wild Nights"—rather than holding Wordsworth's "emotion recollected in tranquility," these poems are vivid, present-moment enactments, and different as they are, there are qualities of speaking they share. The best descriptive poetry falls also into this category, I believe. What Pablo Neruda once referred to as "the furious blood" of his poems makes not only the poems of love, anger, and political rage swell with the vision of genius, but also his poems on tomatoes and wristwatches. Poems of strong feeling flood, overspill; however much the poet may have worked them, they taste of the unrestrainable, of outburst.

Two ways of speaking, singly or together, create this effect. The first is the music of forceful repetition, both in rhythms and words. Anaphora—repetition at a line's or sentence's beginning—is especially pervasive: strong feeling stutters forward. The second is the frequent inclusion of lists and the mounding up of detail; here, strength of emotion bursts forth as if by its own abundance. What poems of this type will not show is markedly visible logopoeia. Passion does not make careful arguments: it declares itself, and that is enough.

Both these earmarks of passionate feeling appear in Sylvia Plath's "Zoo Keeper's Wife." The poem begins with the lines, "I can stay awake all night, if need be— / Cold as an eel, without eyelids." Here is its final stanza:

How our courtship lit the tindery cages—
Your two-horned rhinoceros opened a mouth
Dirty as a bootsole and big as a hospital sink
For my cube of sugar: its bog breath
Gloved my arm to the elbow.
The snails blew kisses like black apples.
Nightly now I flog apes owls bears sheep
Over their iron stile. And still don't sleep.

Plath's rage unleashes itself in a rush of accumulating surreal detail, both distorting and accurate; her parade of animals has a nighmare's wildness of reach. The distinctive music of emotion-driven poetry is present as well—these lines press forward with percussive, insistent rhythm; hard consonants clip; alliteration and assonance thicken until the words reel. Then the blunt rhyme of the final two lines slams the poem shut, violence of feeling palpable in its every part.

A different emotion appears in the closing section of Theodore Roethke's "The Shape of the Fire." Here, at the end of a long poem that has been wildly disordered, the healing power of the natural replenishes the psyche in a wealth of closely focused images, in the anaphoric murmur of infinitive verbs, and in the more subtle, but still audible, rhyme of both the first and last words in each of the final two lines. The poem unfurls wonder, gratitude, the amazement that fulfillment is possible:

> To have the whole air!
> The light, the full sun
> Coming down on the flowerheads,
> The tendrils turning slowly,
> A slow snail-lifting, liquescent;
> To be by the rose
> Rising slowly out of its bed,
> Still as a child in its first loneliness;
> To see cyclamen veins become clearer in early sunlight,
> And mist lifting out of the brown cattails;
> To stare into the after-light, the glitter left on the lake's surface,
> When the sun has fallen behind a wooded island;
> To follow the drops sliding from a lifted oar,
> Held up, while the rower breathes, and the small boat drifts
>   quietly shoreward;
> To know that light falls and fills, often without our knowing,

As an opaque vase fills to the brim from a quick pouring,
Fills and trembles at the edge yet does not flow over,
Still holding and feeding the stem of the contained flower.

Repetition and list can also be used to convey extremity of feeling within the context of its restraint. In a mastery probably unchosen, but no less achieved, what we feel in such poems is the effort it costs the writer simply to speak at all. Elizabeth Bishop's villanelle "One Art" is a consummate example, a calm and formal listing of losses— houses, rivers, a mother's watch, the poem's simple, heartbreaking "you"—in which the poet's control is broken by only a single moment of struggle: "It's evident / the art of losing's not too hard to master / though it may look like (*Write* it!) like disaster."

Another poet of restraint is Constantin Cavafy. Homosexual love and the condition of religious or linguistic outcastness (both historically and in his own early twentieth-century Alexandria) occupy much of his work. His sonnet "Hidden Things" is a work stripped even more bare than Bishop's villanelle; it may be no accident that both these poets chose to work frequently within the binding framework of form. As with Bishop, a keening comes through the poet's ostensible control: even amid irony, Cavafy's quiet repetitions communicate the strict fierceness of his grief.

Hidden Things

From all I did and all I said
let no one try to find out who I was.
An obstacle was there that changed the pattern
of my actions and the manner of my life.
An obstacle was often there
to stop me when I'd begin to speak.
From my most unnoticed actions,
my most veiled writing—

from these alone will I be understood.
But maybe it isn't worth so much concern,
so much effort to discover who I really am.
Later, in a more perfect society,
someone else made just like me
is certain to appear and act freely.

(trans. Edmund Keeley and Philip Sherrard)

▾   ▾   ▾   ▾   ▾

Next comes the concentration of narrative, in which event itself is the sinew that moves a poem forward. Storytelling, like rhetoric, pulls us in through the cognitive mind as much as through the emotions. It answers both our curiosity and our longing for shapely forms: our profound desire to know what happens, and our persistent hope that what happens will somehow make sense. Narrative instructs us in both these hungers and their satisfaction, teaching us to perceive and to relish the arc of moments and the arc of lives. If shapeliness is illusion, it is one we require—it shields against arbitrariness and against chaos's companion, despair. And story, like all the forms of concentration, connects. It brings us to a deepened coherence with the world of others and also within the many levels of the self.

Much of the cultural work once performed by poetic narrative has been taken on by film and works in prose; one reason will be explored later in this book. Yet story remains a basic human path toward the discovery and ordering of meaning and beauty, and the narrative lyric, especially, continues to flourish. An example is Tess Gallagher's poem written after the death of her father, "Black Silk":

She was cleaning—there is always
that to do—when she found,

at the top of the closet, his old
silk vest. She called me
to look at it, unrolling it carefully
like something live
might fall out. Then we spread it
on the kitchen table and smoothed
the wrinkles down, making our hands
heavy until its shape against Formica
came back and the little tips
that would have pointed to his pockets
lay flat. The buttons were all there.
I held my arms out and she
looped the wide armholes over
them. "That's one thing I never
wanted to be," she said, "a man."
I went into the bathroom to see
how I looked in the sheen and
sadness. Wind chimes
off-key in the alcove. Then her
crying so I stood back in the sink-light
where the porcelain had been staring. Time
to go to her, I thought, with that
other mind, and stood still.

The energies of poetry's concentrations do not exist in isolation
from one another, and this poem is suffused with sound and images,
with precisely deployed grammar and passionate feeling. The vest—
what is still here, with each of its buttons intact—is made present with
all the sensuous particularity of the mind of image. The grammatical
concentration of rhetoric is here as well: we are left to infer the vast-
ness of what is not here—the father—solely through the subjunctive
phrase, "the little tips that *would have* pointed to his pockets." Then
there is the subtle displacement of "like something live might fall
out," in whose colloquial diction we hear the echo of this grown

daughter's childhood. Reading the words, we think first of what moths or spiders might live on the high shelves of a rarely opened closet; only afterward do we realize the deeper resonance of the phrase.

Still, "Black Silk" is not so much about grief in its overwhelming first arrival as it is about how we continue living with grief once it has entered our lives in an irreversible way. That is why the heart of the poem lies in narrative, in its telling of what this mother and daughter do and fail to do. By describing without commentary or judgment what is found, what is said, what is thought and done, Gallagher succeeds in being both tactful and entirely revealing. Such reticence is one of narrative's strengths: story, at its best, becomes a canvas to which the reader as well as the writer must bring the full range of memory, intellect, and imaginative response. The best stories are almost mythlike in their ability to support alternative readings, different conclusions—for instance, nothing within this poem tells us that it is about a nuclear family, and the poem is equally moving if read in other ways. The words of a poem are not ends, but means into an exploration without limit.

Narrative carries the knowledge of our alteration through the shifting currents of circumstance and time. What then is the core perception of "Black Silk"? It is a poem about the ways that love both binds and changes us over time, and about the solitude the grief of maturity finally brings. In separation from the father lies an irrevocable separation from the mother as well: holding out her arms, the poet is given not the comfort of familial love, but what Gallagher has described elsewhere as "the arm holes of absence." This daughter who slips her body into roles the mother would not choose is also a daughter who experiences the material weight of each side of the family drama. She slips, too, into the word-sewn fabric of her own life—its stories of luminous sheen, sadness, loneliness, anger; its bright self-knowledge and dark threads of strength.

▾   ▾   ▾   ▾   ▾

THE FINAL poetic concentration to consider is voice—not the grammatical voice of rhetoric, but the lived inhabitance a good poem gives off. Voice is not a matter of subject, nor of the activity a poem undertakes; it is another level of content, equally essential to a poem's realization, infusing each choice and gesture a poem makes. Voice is the underlying style of being that creates a poem's rounding presence, making it continuous, idiosyncratic, and recognizable.

A person's heard voice is replete with information. So it is with the voice of a poem, directing us in myriad ways into the realm it inhabits—a realm more or less formal, more or less argumentative, more or less emotional, linear, textured. As we gauge a person's kindness by tone, regardless of what she is saying, we similarly recognize a poem's tenderness or harshness toward the world around it; its engagement or detachment; whether it is ironic, comic, fantastic, serious, compassionate, irreverent, or philosophical. We intuit these things as a dog intuits another dog's friendly or challenging disposition.

Voice in this sense is the body language of a poem—the part that cannot help but reveal what it is. Everything that has gone into making us who we are is held there. Yet we also speak of writers "finding their voice." The phrase is both meaningful and odd, a perennial puzzle: how can we "find" what we already use? The answer lies, paradoxically, in the quality of listening that accompanies self-aware speech: singers, to stay in tune, must hear not only the orchestral music they sing with, but also themselves. Similarly, writers who have "found a voice" are those whose ears turn at once inward and outward, both toward their own nature, thought patterns, and rhythms, and toward those of the culture at large.

Sometimes, as with Emily Dickinson or William Blake, a writer's ear will lean far toward the inner; the risk then is that his or her voice will be incomprehensible to others, at least for a time. But there is risk, too, for the writer who turns only outward, toward the speech and thought of the commons: such language, though comprehensible, has not been dipped in the stubborn ink of one person's uniqueness. Even the ostensibly "plain" language of early William Carlos Williams, of William Bronk, or of Robert Creeley is in some way also a heightening, a paring and framing—that is what makes their words poems. The effects of voice can be seen most easily, though, at the other end of the spectrum, as in Gerard Manley Hopkins's "Carrion Comfort":

> Not, I'll not, carrion comfort, Despair, not feast on thee;
> Not untwist—slack as they may be—these last strands of man
> In me ór, most weary, cry *I can no more*. I can;
> Can something, hope, wish day come, not choose not to be.
>
> But ah, but O thou terrible, why wouldst thou rude on me
> Thy wring-world right foot rock? lay a lionlimb against me? scan
> With darksome devouring eyes my bruisèd bones? and fan,
> O in turns of tempest, me heaped there; me frantic to avoid thee
>   and flee?
>
> Why? That my chaff might fly; my grain lie, sheer and clear.
> Nay in all that toil, that coil, since (seems) I kissed the rod,
> Hand rather, my heart lo! lapped strength, stole joy, would
>   laugh, cheer.
>
> Cheer whóm though? Thé hero whose héaven-handling flúng me,
>   fóot tród
> Me? or mé that fóught him? O whích one? is it eách one? That níght,
>   that year
> Of now done darkness I wretch lay wrestling with (my God!)
>   my God.

The poem's rhetorical frame is an address, directed to the second-person Despair; yet however rooted it is in the gestures of speech, this sonnet's language comes to a music wholly original and poetry-born. Halting and rushing at once, inventive, pressured, elliptical, from its first phrase the poem stands removed from the ordinary orders of meaning. Yet once the reader agrees to its ways, she can imagine no other vessel for what is here said; disrupted word order, new compounds, and self-correction become the marks of the onslaught of which the poem speaks. This is language that marries rhetorical, intellectual, and theologically inquiring mind with the thick-laid sounds and images of the poetry of feeling. It is an alchemy not seen before, made by the genius of Hopkins's concentration.

Though voice dominates in "Carrion Comfort," every realized poem has a carriage unmistakably its own. One of the ways we come to recognize the work of individual writers is by developing a sense for their characteristic ways of addressing the world and of moving a poem. Recall Elizabeth Bishop's similes, honed by the self-correction she may have learned from Hopkins; Dickinson's staccato rhythms of insight; Jorie Graham's fracturings, gaps, and mixing of abstraction with concrete detail ("the sleek whiskey-colored slice of time"); Galway Kinnell's encyclopedic lyrical reach and the occasional turns of humor in even his most serious poems. Each of these modes of speaking both mirrors and creates a self—at least the self of the poems and, quite possibly, as Yeats implied in the quatrain quoted earlier, of the life as well.

▼   ▼   ▼   ▼   ▼

No MATTER how carefully we read or how much attention we bring to bear, a good poem can never be completely entered, completely known. If it is the harvest of true concentration, it will know more than can be said in any other way. And because it thinks by music and image, by story and passion and voice, poetry can do what other forms of thinking cannot: approximate the actual flavor of life, in which subjective and objective become one, in which conceptual mind and the inexpressible presence of things become one.

Letting this wideness of being into ourselves, as readers or as writers, while staying close to the words themselves, we begin to find in poems a way of entering both language and being on their own terms. Poetry leads us into the self, but also away from it. Transparency is part of what we seek in art, and in art's mind of concentration that is both capacious and focused. Free to turn inward and outward, free to remain still and wondering amid the mysteries of mind and world, we arrive, for a moment, at a kind of fullness that overspills into everything. One breath taken completely; one poem, fully written, fully read—in such a moment, anything can happen. The pressed oil of words can blaze up into music, into image, into the heart and mind's knowledge. The lit and shadowed places within us can be warmed.

The Question of Originality

▼   ▼   ▼   ▼   ▼   ▼   ▼   ▼   ▼

IMAGINE walking down a city street, distracted, hurrying, hot, and seeing, in the mass of people about a half block ahead, a friend. From a glimpse of dark hair and perhaps the dipping motion of one shoulder, how easy it is to recognize a person we know amid the rest. Physical being is effortlessly original: we can press our fingertips against any surface and leave an unmistakable signature. Yet few writers seem able to press that same individuality unblurred into words. A question, then, is how does a poet enfold into language the singularity that marks each living creature and object of the world and also those works of art we most admire?

ANY thinking about originality needs first to acknowledge its two faces. When we call a work "original," we point to the way it is irreducibly and creatively itself—individual, recognizable, and distinct. Sometimes, though, we use the word to refer to innovation, to some quality within it previously unseen, while at other times we mean more the idea of authentic presence—the idea that a work, like a person, is original not because it is new in subject matter or technique but because it has the uniqueness that moistens and flares in all embodied being. These aspects of originality are not entirely separate, but they are also not the same. From its beginning, the concept reaches in both directions.

The word *original* comes from the Latin verb *oriri*, "to rise," which refers especially to the rising of the sun and moon; but it reaches English through the noun *origo*—the rising of a spring from its source in the earth. Each root contributes its flavor. The first is intermittent and repeated, the second a continuous flow. One offers a sense of time that is cyclical, arriving and leaving; the other is timeless. One tells the old debate of light and darkness; the other murmurs of a sustaining essence, water's steady, unaccountable emergence from rocky earth. The paradox of originality is that it points both to the newly appearing and to a continuance free of time and says within itself that they are one.

Though from different roots, the Sanskrit word translated as "origination," *samutpāda*, contains the same motion as the Latin: *sam* means "completely," *ut* is "up," and *pāda*, "created." Its Tibetan counterpart, *'byung-ba* (pronounced jung-wa), means similarly "to arise." These words hold the insight, familiar from both Buddhism and physics, that the world we think we know is made up—and in that phrase a certain momentum continues: the creative is buoyant, it climbs. The founding metaphor comes from plants: roots go down, stems and leaves ascend. Such basic perceptions form an underground river, always available, from which we draw both our world and our words; in its fluid and fluent waters, meaning begins.

EVERY originality mirrors the generative perception found first within individual words; to understand how new thought is made, it may be useful to look first at this most basic construction of meaning. Linguists say that each new object or idea is named by stitching it metaphorically into the web of the physical, which needs no explanation; one good account of the process is George Lakoff and Mark Johnson's *Metaphors We Live By*. From the basic experiences of "rising," "falling," "more," "less," "hard," "sweet," and "bitter," Lakoff and Johnson suggest, we create our verbal and mental worlds. Emerson too described the process: all language, he wrote, is "fossil poetry." The understanding of one thing in terms of another is actively, invisibly at work in the formation of any word; language begins in the facts of physical life, but takes flight by the same creative strategies found in poems. We have already seen this: in the leap from the literal springs of the earth to the idea of originality, a swerve into the connecting mind of likeness has taken place.

In everyday speech, this creative interweaving is hidden, a shadow activity mostly ignored. In poetry, though, the rich history of words' creation is precipitated back into view. A good poem draws on the originality hidden at language-making's core and also replenishes that originality. It flenses the dulling familiarity from words, allowing them to gleam as they did when first made.

Both the reading and the writing of poems explore one thing by means of another; each draws on a fundamentally metaphorical mind in order to reach toward the new. We turn to Shakespeare's sonnets to learn not about Shakespeare's life but about our own. The beauty, feeling, and understanding they hold throw off a continuing brightness, and within its circle the hand holding the page is also freshly lit. The writing of poetry, too, is a metaphorical endeavor. The writer reaches by means of language into the outer world—the world of things, and also of words themselves and their storehoused wisdom—in order to question and discover the texture and substance of being. An oar moves a boat by entering what lies outside it. A poem, like an oar, extends inner life into the waters of story and things, of language and music. There we in turn are changed, moved by the encounter's supporting buoyancy, and also its useful resistance.

It is no accident then that we speak of a body of knowledge: thought constructs itself in the world of material objects, fragrances, and sensual presence in time. Consciousness itself was made possible, linguists suggest, only when language constructed a metaphorical "space" in which it could live. Symbolic and image-based language is as much an element of our psyches as the sea is of our blood. Yet because it is so deeply our own substance, the actual workings of creative understanding remains mysterious: we cannot escape from thought to view it in any objective way. To walk on fresh lava is possible once it has hardened and cooled, but the volcano's core remains an untraversable fire.

▼   ▼   ▼   ▼   ▼

ARTISTS freely admit their ignorance concerning creative insight. A letter said to be Mozart's describes it this way:

> When I am, as it were, completely myself, entirely alone, and of good cheer—say, travelling in a carriage, or walking after a good meal, or during the night when I cannot sleep; it is on such occasions that my ideas flow best and most abundantly. *Whence* and *how* they come, I know not; nor can I force them. . . .
>
> When I proceed to write, the committing to paper is done quickly enough, for everything is, as I said before, already finished. . . . But why my productions take from my hand that particular form and style that makes them *Mozartish,* and different from the works of other composers, is probably owing to the same cause which renders my nose so large or so aquiline, or, in short, makes it Mozart's, and different from those of other people. For I really do not study or aim at originality.
>
> *(trans. Edward Holmes)*

Art-making begins when the mind enters a condition different from everyday, discursive thinking—the condition Mozart called being completely himself and I have called concentration. In this state, what arises feels less *made* than *gift*, and Mozart's indifference to originality is widely echoed. Even the most revolutionary writers deny any conscious effort toward uniqueness. Thus, Gertrude Stein:

> You will write if you will write without thinking of the result in terms of a result, but think of the writing in terms of discovery, which is to say that creation must take place between the pen and the paper, not before in a thought or afterwards in a recasting. Yes, before in a thought, but not in careful thinking. It will come if it is there and if you will let it come, and if you have anything you will get a sudden creative recognition. . . . The great thing is not ever to think about form but let it come. Does that sound strange from me? They have accused me of thinking about nothing else. Do you see the real joke? It is the critics who have really thought about form always, and I have thought about—writing!

Then there is Pablo Picasso:

> The artist is a receptacle of emotions come from no matter where: from the sky, the earth, a piece of paper, a passing figure, a cobweb. This is why one must not discriminate between things. There is no rank among them. One must take one's good where one finds it. . . .
>
> When we invented cubism, we had no intention of inventing cubism, but simply of expressing what was in us. Nobody drew up a program of action, and though our friends the poets followed our efforts attentively, they never dictated to us. The young painters of today often outline a program for themselves to follow and try to do their assignments correctly like well-behaved schoolboys.
>
> The painter passes through states of fullness and of emptying. That is the whole secret of art.

(trans. Brewster Ghiselin)

And Walt Whitman:

> The greatest poet has less a marked style and is more the free channel of himself. He swears to his art, I will not be meddlesome, I will not have in my writing any elegance or effect or originality to hang in the way between me and the rest like curtains. I will have nothing hang in the way, not the richest curtains. What I tell I tell for precisely what it is.

Intention, then, does not matter; the artist's concern is the task at hand and how to pursue it. Wallace Stevens put it this way: Anyone with a passion for truth will of necessity be original.

PASSION for truth is an idea with more than one face. It includes the determination to look closely and long, to be unsatisfied with the secondhand and assumption. It includes the emotions and the body, acknowledging that the writer's whole being is the instrument of perception, not only the mind. It also hints that only the hunger for something beyond the personal will allow a writer to break free of one major obstacle to originality—the fear of self-revelation.

The Buddhist psychology system known as Abhidharma includes a list of five great fears—fear of death, fear of the loss of livelihood, fear of unusual states of consciousness, fear of loss of reputation, and fear of speaking before a public assembly. Each can play a part in tempering the glimmerings of original thought, but public speech is the particular demon of writers. Whether autobiographical or seemingly fictional, every sentence exposes the writer to a fear of social rejection that the Abhidharma ranks alongside fear of death.

The reluctance to expose untempered thought is well schooled: a good part of childhood is spent discovering what is acceptable, what not. We learn to speak and act in ways that will receive favor, learn the punishments and rewards by which the conventions of society are enforced. Even in the realm of biology, self-revelation holds risk. Animals find safety in camouflage and blending in among others: the antelope that stands out is the one that is taken. History, mythology, and folktales are filled with stories of people punished for saying the truth. Only the Fool, exempt from society's rules, is allowed to speak with complete freedom.

Right speech is at the core of a right life. Buddhism teaches that the quality of one's speech is a part of liberation's path; the Bill of Rights lists speaking freely as fundamental to democracy's health; Judeo-Christian tradition commands us not to lie. A matured truthfulness is what every culture asks of its wise elders. But the very existence of formal religious injunctions toward honest speech confirms that self-revelation is no easy task. Leaving the refuge of silence demands the willingness to be seen, to be judged. It demands that we turn away from our desires to please, to fit in, to spare the feelings of those we love, and also from our desire to create a shapeliness that does not reflect how awkward, unfinished, and ambivalent actual experience is. For the writer, the person of public speech, it demands risking the fates of Mandelstam or Horace, Sor Juana or Christopher Smart. Or more likely, risking failure more minor: boredom, triviality, confusion. Risking seeing that we are lesser beings than we had hoped.

LET US grant that a writer takes up the challenge: she will speak with her own voice, he will pursue truth. How is it done? One hint is found in the words of Mozart's letter, "When I am, as it were, completely myself, entirely alone." Solitude, whether endured or embraced, is a necessary gateway to original thought: only a writer who fears neither abandonment nor self-presence can write without distortion. Virginia Woolf's room of one's own and five hundred pounds a year are a good start, though many have managed without them. But even beyond the circumstances that material independence bestows, the writer must find the door to an inner seclusion. Only a willingness to live truly apart permits what Emily Dickinson once described to her niece: "Just a turn of the doorknob, and there lies freedom."

Originality requires the aptitude for exile. The physical exile of writers from Po Chü-i to Joseph Brodsky and, in her own way, Dickinson, is the outcome of their willingness to travel first the roads of independent mind. Such independence may be of ideas, or it may be of style; in the end, the two are the same. As is the result: a solitude that, however difficult, is also held in affection—even if an affection sometimes mixed.

But the world and its ways must also be held in affection: each new work arises within a tradition and can be received only within that tradition's modes. If a writer is to speak meaningfully, she may stretch communal understandings, but at least some listeners must be able to follow her words. Even if those listeners are only a handful, it is they who will keep the work available until broader recognition arrives.

Artists with a truly idiosyncratic aesthetic are rare, but the issue touches all to some degree. Every writer draws on the great works of the past: they have given her or him everything. But what they give is also by definition the already known. The writer desiring a free ear and eye cannot fall completely into the available knowledge and syntax or into any inherited discovery of poetry's powers. Instead he must learn the tradition and rise above it, absorb and then abandon what has come before. Bernard Berenson's definition of genius in painting comes to mind: "the capacity for a productive reaction against one's training."

Each writer fully awake to her task rediscovers and remakes poetry's language, plunging it into immediacy, into the perceptions and diction flowing within this moment. Originality can then mean altering the course of a tradition's river: broadening its banks through new usage, pulling in a new tributary of dialect. Or it can mean simply—as with Dickinson, for example—changing it through the voice of a deeply eccentric muse. But originality can also be found when the water of common language bites more deeply into the groundrock of experience, revealing freshly its buried layers.

PART OF any good artist's work is to find a right balance between the independence born of willing solitude and the ability to speak for and to others. Neitzsche's "Three Metamorphoses" offers some insight into how this is done. The philosopher describes three stages through which the spirit must pass before it can truly serve. First it must become a camel, then the camel a lion, and finally the lion a child. The camel, who feeds on acorns and grasses and the hunger for truth, is a being who has agreed to bear the weight of the world, to carry the difficult forward by her own obstinate strength. For a writer, this stage represents the willingness to be instructed by things as they are, to enter into tradition and culture and be affected by the issues and hardships of common human life. Having accomplished this task, Nietzsche writes, the spirit needs to turn lionlike and slay the dragon of external values, whose every scale is a golden plaque reading "Thou shalt." Here, a writer steps outside received opinion and enters creative freedom, beginning to find his resources within. It is a stage described also in a saying from Zen: "If you meet the Buddha on the road, kill him." But rebellion and independence are still not enough. The lion too must give way, and become a child: only in a child's forgetting and innocence can a truly new spirit come into the world. This is the beginning of genuinely original creation, the moment in which the writer can turn at last toward the work without preconception, without any motive beyond knowing the taste of what is.

A poem by the T'ang dynasty poet Wang Wei offers a glimpse of such a state:

In my middle years I became fond of the Way
And made my home in the foothills of South Mountain.
When the spirit moves me I go off by myself
To see things that I alone must see.
I follow the stream to the source,
And sitting there, watch for the moment
When clouds rise up. Or I may meet a woodsman;
We talk and laugh and forget about going home.

(trans. Tenshin Reb Anderson)

Predetermined desire, including the desire for independence, could only obstruct this sage's path. Any effort toward a particular end would be objectifying, dividing the poet from his experience. Wang Wei cultivates the mind of openness, in which stream and cloud may take their own paths and there is room, too, for the human. The creativity of such a mind is not concerned with any form of deliberate making—a quiet and full attentiveness allows each moment to reveal what is called "original mind." And though the poem shows most clearly Wang Wei's childlike spirit, both camel and lion are also here. Each successive stage is not abandoned, but integrated into the next.

Creative attention is forged not only of openness. The earliest writerly advice of classical Roman literature is Cato the Elder's *Res tene, verba sequentur,* which translates roughly, "Just hang on, the words will follow." Patience, even stubbornness, are necessary traits for a writer—though a stubbornness permeable, turned outward as much as inward, faithful and transparent to the world. Wang Wei follows the stream to its source, then sits down to see what arrives; Picasso's artist is the receptacle of cobwebs and passing clouds. What crops up in our lives matters—it is the substance we think with and the face of what we will become. "Perception is not whimsical, but fatal," Emerson wrote. To meet the incidental with the same intense gaze we bring to the chosen objects of our attention is a further gate to original thought.

"Behind each jewel are three thousand sweating horses" is another call for persistence, this time from Zen. Good writers undertake the work of those horses, in each moment's effort and in the long apprenticeship that muscles the tongue with words as a dancer's barre work muscles her legs and back with movement. Learning the hard-won repertory of craft is also a part of originality—only the presence of many possibilities allows a writer to see which may lead toward the new. Plenitude calls forth plenitude, of the world and of the mind.

▾   ▾   ▾   ▾   ▾

Poetic originality appears not only as new content or diction but also in the development of new techniques and forms. For investigating the process of aesthetic change, one clear example is the emergence of free verse. How did the break with regular forms occur, and what does the answer reveal of the ways that art arrives at the new?

In the largest context, free verse flows from poetry's shift from orality to literacy, as a later chapter will explore; still, it entered nineteenth-century literature from two distinct, identifiable sources. In English, the free-verse tradition begins with Whitman. (Christopher Smart's earlier usage remained an anomaly, without influence on other writers until rediscovered in our own time.) In French poetry, roughly thirty years after *Leaves of Grass* we find *vers libre*'s appearance in Arthur Rimbaud's *Illuminations*. Each book has been described as a radical break in aesthetic practice, yet when looked at more closely, the evolutionary development of each becomes clear. That the same "invention" occurred twice within a few decades also hints that it was not born solely of a solitary inspiration free of context.

Whitman's precedents are not hard to find. A sinuous blank verse goes back to Milton, but Whitman's primary model was the King James Bible, particularly the prose verses of the Psalms. Their form, known as verset, arose as an accident of translation, an attempt to mirror the cadences of the original Hebrew Psalms in English prose. We find verset poetry as early as Thomas à Kempis's fifteenth-century *Imitations of Christ;* later it appears in Smart's *Jubilate Agno,* Friedrich Hölderlin's *Hyperion,* and the work of the Polish poet Adam Mickiewicz. That English-language free verse came into wider use only after Whitman stems in part from the overwhelming power of *Leaves of Grass* itself, in part from the model Whitman offered for a uniquely "American" voice. *Leaves of Grass* can also be seen as answering the Romantics' call for a poetry less artificial and more democratic, one reflective of both common speech and the natural world. Though every poem has a form, form that alters with each moment's needs is in tune with the rejection of Church and King that epitomizes the eighteenth century's revolutions. And though resistance to authority's forms continues to evolve, one of its apexes can surely be found in the social anarchist movements of the twentieth century's opening decades—the period in which free verse and nonrepresentational art also took hold.

Rimbaud's vers libre, like Whitman's line, has clear historical roots. Modernist individualism begins in French philosophy. Further, just as an excess of aristocracy called forth political revolution, so an excess of reified formalism in classical French poetry called forth free verse. As with Whitman, translation played a part. Given the ornate metrics and rhyme schemes required for "proper" verse, maintaining both meaning and correct form in a translation was almost impossible, and poems from other languages came to be rendered instead by prose "trots." Before long, writers began to experiment with "pseudo-translated" work, and in 1827 Aloysius Bertrand conceived of the prose poem form made famous later by Charles Baudelaire, during the years Whitman first put forward *Leaves of Grass.* Rimbaud's free verse was not a large step from this prepared ground.

Chance is fundamental to the workings of the creative mind. To say that external influences played a role in the development of free verse does not diminish Whitman's and Rimbaud's achievement—an artist's originality lies in seeing which of chance's gifts might be of use. Something that is only "different" is not yet art. The accidental discovery must still be turned to meaning, the unlikely juxtaposition made into exuberant connection. Whitman's and Rimbaud's originality lies less in their break with tradition than in the unexpectedly fertile beauty each made by following the breath of a thought where it leads. The power of that discovery, iconoclastic and democratic, remains restless, supple, and alive.

There are poets who bring to the field of language new words, new musics, new orders. Hopkins, John Berryman, and more recent experimental poets have left recognizable marks on the ways we hear and feel language in poems. Other poets' originality lies elsewhere: reading the poems of Elizabeth Bishop or Robinson Jeffers, it is a style of consciousness rather than of language we see most in an altered light, some shadowed corner of experience newly illumined and made perceptible by words. But syntax and form are also worldview; a poem's perception and its linguistic surface are inseparably fused. If they are not, the poem's possible discoveries will be squandered, falling into either the mannered or incoherence.

▾　　▾　　▾　　▾　　▾

Eliot suggested we cannot judge our contemporaries' greatness. *Is it genuine?* is the only gauge he felt appropriate to the work of one's own time. He defined that quality with another question: "Has this poet something to say, a little different from what anyone has said before, and has he found, not only a different way of saying it, but *the* different way of saying it which expresses the difference in what he is saying?" The statement seems equally useful as a description of originality: new language and vision yoked in a marriage of equals.

Eliot said something else as well: Bad poets imitate, great poets steal. Such "borrowing" may seem at first the opposite of originality, yet much is revealed about creative change when we recognize art as an ancient bazaar in which the same pieces of jewelry are continually stolen, polished up, and resold. Poetic song itself has its mythological beginning in an act of theft, as we will later see.

Before the invention of photography, copying was an integral part of every visual artist's training. The purpose was not just to make exemplary works more widely available for study—in the process of making a copy, it was understood, new forms of vision could arise. As Adam Gopnik recounts in his essay "St. Peter's Feet and Rembrandt's Fountain" (in *The New Yorker*, July 4, 1988), copying was done within the understanding that "making comes before meaning"; a copy was to be faithful, but not mechanical. Seemingly accidental shifts in focus during the process became steps by which major changes in art could occur. Michelangelo, copying a fresco by Masaccio, ignored Masaccio's major discovery—the use of perspective in rendering feet—and concentrated instead on the drape of the clothing of a figure of St. Peter. Gopnik tells us that the resulting work offers, for the first time in Western painting, a seemingly three-dimensional, self-supporting figure.

An essay by Theodore Roethke, "How to Write Like Somebody Else," chronicles Roethke's practice of imitating poets he admired. It too recalls that conscious imitation was a common procedure in the past and recommends emulation as one of the great methods of developing craft. If a poet has something of his own to say, it will come through, Roethke suggests. The very support of tradition and the model of another writer enables a writer to be "more himself—or more than himself."

This is one paradox of originality: the willingness to become transparent, to offer oneself to the Other, whether in the world of things or of art, leads toward rather than away from individuality of expression. The originality born of imitation also makes clear how often individuality reveals itself in the passionate details rather than in larger artistic ambitions. There are relatively few essential themes in human life, yet their exploration is endless. Small differences not only matter, they are the mark of a particularized occupancy of self and world.

New writers soon learn Ezra Pound's injunction "Make it new," which is itself a variation of Tolstoy's "Make it strange." Both are useful phrases, pointing to the necessity for a vision and language stripped clean of convention. But "make it new" leans too strongly, perhaps, toward the idea of innovation; a writer ripens by developing a richer, more complex sense of the original and its ways.

American culture loves change; both supermarket and art gallery equate the new with the improved. Improvement is modernism's project; the driving force of Western thought since the Enlightenment, in many realms it has served humankind well. But Bernard Berenson, in *Italian Painters of the Renaissance*, warns of what he calls a "secret preference" in Western culture for what is new, individual, and one's own, over even the beautiful and the good. Such an attitude, he points out, leads as readily to artistic decline as to achievement.

There are other paths. In classical Japanese literature, the highest value was not the creation of the new, but the ability to compress within brief written expression the greatest possible resonance of emotion and perception. Individuality of feeling mattered immensely, but individuality of expression would have been found bizarre by these writers. Over the thousand years between the late eighth century's *Manyōshū* anthology and the appearance of Bashō, poetic diction and strategies changed little, yet the poems themselves changed deeply. There are problems inherent in such a conservative aesthetic—

problems of staleness and repetitive feeling, of an almost mechanical juggling of familiar imagery—but any set of artistic values can produce bad writing. Good poets leap over the pitfalls of the tradition in which they practice.

"Make it yours" is not so memorable as "make it new." If "make it new" remains vivid and awake, it is because the mind leaps from its literal meaning to a more complex understanding: to the wellspring, outside of time, that brims at novelty's feet. Such shadow presences and understandings keep language vital. Within the new is the old—there is, even in "make it new," an "it" already present to be made over. What we discover, we merely remove the cover from; the image, form, or idea has always been there, hidden by our common agreements about reality until an original way of looking peels it into view.

▾   ▾   ▾   ▾   ▾

Some artistic discoveries are rooted in their birthplace and cannot survive translation. Only a faint echo of Hopkins's sprung rhythms, for instance, can pass through that door. But other originalities startle past time, past language:

> You should study the green mountains, using numerous worlds as your standards. You should clearly examine the green mountains walking and your own walking. You should also examine walking backward and backward walking, and investigate the fact that walking forward and backward has never stopped since the very moment before form arose. . . .
>
> Green mountains master walking and eastern mountains master traveling on water. . . . Don't slander by saying that a green mountain cannot walk and an eastern mountain cannot travel on water. When your understanding is shallow, you doubt the phrase, "Green mountains are walking." When your learning is immature, you are shocked by the words "flowing mountains." . . .

All beings do not see mountains and rivers in the same way. Some beings see water as a jeweled ornament, but they do not see jeweled ornaments as water. What in the human realm corresponds to their water? We only see their jeweled ornaments as water. . . . Thus the views of all beings are not the same. You should question this matter now. Are there many ways to see one thing, or is it a mistake to see many forms as one thing? . . .

When we think about the meaning of this, it seems that there is water for various beings, but there is no original water—there is no water common to all types of beings. But water for these various beings does not depend on mind or body, does not arise from actions, does not depend on self or other. Water's freedom depends only on water.

(trans. adapted from Kazuaki Tanahashi and Arnold Kotler)

These are not the words of a contemporary deconstructionist, though this is language that does indeed deconstruct. They are taken from the "Mountains and Rivers Sutra," written by the Japanese Zen master Eihei Dōgen in the first part of the thirteenth century.

"It is not only that there is water in the world," Dōgen wrote,

but there is a world in water. . . . When you investigate the flowing of a handful of water and the not-flowing of it, full mastery of all things is instantly present.

And there are mountains hidden in treasures. There are mountains hidden in swamps. There are mountains hidden in the sky. There are mountains hidden in mountains. There are mountains hidden in hiddenness. This is complete understanding.

An ancient Buddha once said, "Mountains are mountains, waters are waters." These words do not mean mountains are mountains; they mean mountains are mountains.

I can think of no more original use of language than this, and no greater insight into what an original seeing is. To understand Dōgen is not easy, yet he tried only to express what he perceived, in words as lucid and explicit as he could find. Even when we fail to understand them, his thoughts haunt. But "There are mountains hidden in mountains, there are mountains hidden in hiddenness" is comprehensible to anyone. It tells of what can be known and of how much escapes our knowing. It tells also where originality can be found. Capturing the mountains that travel on rivers and hide in the sky and in swamps, that hide above all in themselves—this is what writers do.

▾   ▾   ▾   ▾   ▾

O RIGINALITY can be hunted. Concentration's deep attentiveness; permeability to accident; persistence; curiosity; a wide vocabulary of outer and inner worlds—these are just a few of the ways. Playfulness and rebelliousness help. Intelligence and seriousness help. Passion. The courage for independence. A knowledge of tradition, perversely, helps.

The avant garde of this century's first decades searched for ways to break free of rational mind and familiar aesthetics. In the desire for a greater transparency to the Other, writers sought willed means for escaping from will. They turned to automatic writing and to the associative, displacing, and condensing processes of dream; to techniques of arbitrary rejuxtapositioning; to the retention of visible gestures of thought and revision in a finished piece; to the intentional inclusion of processes of chance. These techniques were practiced deliberately at first, but later as strategies taken for granted within the mainstream of writing. They invite the mind to a widened sense of the possible, opening it to the fragrant, stored oils of the unconscious.

Learning to trust the possible and to accept what arises, to welcome surprise and the ways of the Trickster, not to censor too quickly—all are lessons necessary for a writer. One can think of these avant-garde strategies as the road of language itself: what arises from them is not different in kind from what happens in writing formal verse, when qualities of sound summon new meaning into the world. It is no coincidence that the avant garde and free verse arrive at roughly the same time. Apparent opposites, the poetics of traditional form and the aesthetics of the arbitrary depend upon the same creative ground: the fertility of chance, of juxtaposing mind.

The other road toward original mind is the road of inner awareness. Its originality comes not from overt intention, but from the thickets and currents of life. Like the road of language, it is traveled each time a writer takes up the pen. Choices of topic, image, and word reflect perfectly the self and all its history; every gesture is a clear lake in whose waters the whole ecology of self and culture swims. Even the workings of chance reveal that self—for contingency is also who we are, inseparable from all that happens and from everything we touch. The writer's offering to originality, then, is a transforming openness: to things, to events, to inner compulsion, to the finest cross-hatched lines of the drawing consciousness makes. Attentiveness may appear to be empty and passive, to be nothing at all, yet under its gaze, everything flowers. "Awakened," Dōgen wrote in a poem, "I hear the one true thing— / Black rain on the roof of Fukakusa temple."

ORIGINALITY lives at the crossroads, at the point where world and self open to each other in transparence in the night rain. There, the plenitude of being comes and goes. Originality summons originality: a work of art that contains the mind of freedom will call forth freedom in others. But originality also asks presence—the willingness to inhabit ourselves amid the uncertain transports and sufferings that are our fate. To feel, and to question feeling; to know, and to agree to wander utterly lost in the dark, where every journey of the soul starts over.

If we demand change too insistently—in art, or in the self—something grows stubborn and digs in its heels. But within presence and a lightness of being, we can open into the new. It may be that originality is simply what you step out of the way of; it is what must come if the old ways are dropped, discarded like clothes. But originality is also a question, a request we make of ourselves and the world. We ask it in the quality of our attention and concentration, and we ask it without expectation of an answer. Such a request, self-raised, self-contained, ripens itself.

To look closely with the attention of questioning changes everything. It is, if undertaken fully, revolutionary. It is what Rainer Maria Rilke's "Archaic Torso of Apollo" is about, with its famous last sentence:

We cannot know his legendary head
with eyes like ripening fruit. And yet his torso
is still suffused with brilliance from inside,
like a lamp, in which his gaze, now turned to low,

gleams in all its power. Otherwise
the curved breast could not dazzle you so, nor could
a smile run through the placid hips and thighs
to that dark center where procreation flared.

Otherwise this stone would seem defaced
beneath the translucent cascade of the shoulders
and would not glisten like a wild beast's fur:

would not, from all the borders of itself,
burst like a star: for here there is no place
that does not see you. You must change your life.

(trans. Stephen Mitchell)

Do not think it an accident that it is Apollo, patron god of poetry, at whose figure Rilke looks. The activity of poetry is to tell us we must change our lives. It does this by posing again and again a question that cannot be answered except with our whole being—body, speech, and mind. What is the nature of this moment? poetry asks, and we have no rest until the question is answered. Then it is asked again. To live in this question is Dōgen's request as well, made in the last three lines of the "Mountains and Rivers Sutra," lines that tell us why the mind of originality is both inexhaustible and always new:

> Therefore, investigate mountains thoroughly. When you investigate mountains thoroughly, this is the work of the mountains. Such mountains and rivers of themselves become sages and teachers.

The World Is Large and Full of Noises:

Thoughts on Translation

*Translation it is that
openeth the window
to let in the light; that
breaketh the shell, that
we may eat the kernel.*

Preface to the King
James Bible

▾ ▾ ▾ ▾ ▾ ▾ ▾ ▾ ▾ ▾

Even the physical embodiment of a sacred text is numinous: it is wrapped in leather or silk, stored in a cupboard used for no other purpose, copied over only by special scribes. It may be raised in both hands as an offering before being opened; it may itself be offered fragrant incense and sweet milk. All written work retains some trace, however faint, of this initial sanctity of the Word: the breath inhabiting Logos and the breath of inspiration are the same, each bringing new life into the empty places of earth. It is no wonder, then, that many different cultural traditions share an ancient prohibition against translation. As George Steiner has pointed out in *After Babel*, if a sacred text has been given to us directly by its divine source, surely it must remain exactly as it first appeared, each word preserved intact for the meaning it may hold. Whether in a sacred text or a contemporary poem, any alteration risks unwittingly discarding some mystery not yet penetrated.

Unease about translation does not just cover the exporting of texts into another language; their importation too can be problematic. Translation's very existence challenges our understanding of what a literary text is. Further, by asserting that things worth knowing exist outside the home culture's boundaries, translation challenges society as a whole. Translated works are Trojan horses, carriers of secret invasion. They open the imagination to new images and beliefs, new modes of thought, new sounds. Mistrust of translation is part of the instinctive immune reaction by which every community attempts to preserve its particular heritage and flavor: to control language is to control thought. The realization lends an extra dimension to the well-known Italian saying, "Traduttore, traditore" (Translator, traitor).

And still, translation occurs, playing an essential role in the innumerable conversations between familiar and strange, native and import, past and future, by which history and culture are made. It is integral to the way seed ideas and language strategies move out into the world, the new contending with the old until the translated works and forms are either rejected or naturalized. After sufficient time, shapes of thought and sound originally alien may themselves become the revered heritage, as certain exotic trees have come to be treasured in their new countries. Consider English literature, built almost entirely on the adopted powers of other traditions. Before the eleventh century's Norman invasion, English poetry relied on alliteration, not rhyme, for its binding sound, and the number of syllables within each metrical foot could vary freely. Yet what English speaker today would call iambic pentameter an imported meter, or think of the sonnet as an Italian form?

The desire to learn what lives within the incomprehensible speech of others is part of the deep-rooted human desire to know always more than we do. Such curiosity will overcome external limits, whatever the authority behind them—that is one lesson of Eden. And if the tale of the apple tells us the cost of such knowledge is death, and the story of Babel says that the price for pride of knowledge is a multiplicity of tongues, both offer no simple punishment. From each story's loss comes a gain: a sorrow, yes, but one that also gives birth to the continuing fertility and richness of this world.

WHAT do poets themselves have to say of translation? On the fifteenth of February, 1924, Rilke inscribed these lines on the copy of *The Duino Elegies* he gave his Polish translator:

Happy are those who know:
Behind all words, the Unsayable stands;
And from that source alone, the Infinite
Crosses over to gladness, and us—

Free of our bridges,
Built with the stone of distinctions;
So that always, within each delight,
We gaze at what is purely single and joined.

With the gift of this poem about words' relationship to the Absolute, Rilke attempted to free his translator from the curse of "traitor." The Infinite comes into being only through the divided world of the particular, the poem says; while lesser, this realm of distinctions remains a realm of gladness, both necessary and good. By acknowledging that every word is both a reflection of his work's original mind and a path toward it, Rilke gave his translator his blessing to do whatever was needed. He offered his full trust that whatever the Polish words, the *Elegies* would remain alive.

The ontological issue at the center of Rilke's poem is this: where does a poem's true being reside? Surely poetry lives in the body of its words, as we live in our human bodies of bone and nerve, muscle and blood. Yet even in writing a poem's first draft, it often seems as if something were already there, which we hunt with words—something like the poem's soul. What else to call that magnetic pull of a destination unknown yet nonetheless present and calling, which causes a writer to accept one arising phrase and reject another, or to delete or alter or expand during revision?

The act of writing is a making, but also a following: of the mystery of source as it emerges into form; of the wisdom of the heart-mind as it encounters the wisdom of language. Translation asks a similar leap of faith. It becomes possible only if we trust that poetry lives both in its words and beyond them, and that at least some portion of this ur-poem can cross the abyss between one verbal body and another.

The Sung dynasty poet Yang Wan-li wrote on this subject as well:

Now, what is poetry? If you say it is simply a matter of words, I will say a good poet gets rid of words. If you say it is simply a matter of meaning, I will say a good poet gets rid of meaning. "But," you ask, "without words and without meaning, where is the poetry?" To this I reply, "Get rid of words and get rid of meaning, and still there is poetry."

(trans. Jonathan Chaves)

Yang argues against any idea of poetry that is unchangeable, unchallengeable, or fixed. In his use of meaning to urge us to pass beyond meaning, in his use of words to pass beyond words, he points to the mode of knowledge described in the Heart Sutra, the central text of Zen: "no eyes, no ears, no nose, no tongue, no body, no mind, no consciousness." The description does not mean that an awakened person is blind, struck deaf, numb to the world, and dumb. Rather, such a person is one who knows the world directly, without mediation, and knows the self in its widest existence, reflected in all things. The poet, too, is free to see with no eyes, to speak with no tongue. Poetry will continue on its own path, untroubled.

From the open spirit of these two passages, translators may take heart. Though I only encountered their words years after undertaking a cotranslation of the work of two classical-era Japanese women poets, I nonetheless found in them a retrospective reassurance, and also a kind of blessing. The old prohibitions live on as a useful self-doubt in the translator, ensuring that original texts be approached with due care. But still the silk ribbons of the home language must be cut, for the work to be read by others.

▾ ▾ ▾ ▾ ▾

K NOWLEDGE is erotic. We see this not only in the Bible's dual use of the term "to know," but also, as classicist Anne Carson has pointed out, in the Homeric verb *mnaomai*, which means both "to hold in attention" and "to woo." What we regard must seduce us, and we it, if we are to continue looking. A great poem creates in its readers the desire to know it more thoroughly, to live with it in intimacy, to join its speaking to their own as fully as possible. We memorize it, recite it over and over, reawaken it with tongue and mind and heart. Many translators describe their first encounter with their chosen authors as a helpless falling in love: a glimpse of a few translated fragments can lead to years of language study in order to hear directly the work's own voice. And in matters of art, it seems, Eros is generous rather than possessive: the translator wants to reciprocate this gift received, to pass the new love on to others—and thus the work of translation begins.

A writer may turn to translating for therapeutic reasons as well, at times for self-cure, at times in the spirit of a physician prescribing for others. The translator-as-patient hopes some power of the original will enter her own work, or else uses translation as a way to keep fit during periods of nonwriting. Robert Lowell names both motivations in his introduction to *Imitations;* it isn't hard to see how the work of that book helped him both develop his range and, at the same time, step a little free of his own preoccupations. Kenneth Rexroth, another poet-translator, describes the curative aspect of translation at its best in his essay "The Poet as Translator": "The writer who can project himself into the exultation of another learns more than the craft of words. He learns the stuff of poetry. It is not just his prosody he keeps alert, it is his heart."

The translator-as-physician, on the other hand, hopes the new work will correct some misdirection or gap he perceives in the literature of his own time and language. Ezra Pound put forward both the troubadors of medieval France and the classical poets of China as good medicine for the lack of vigor he saw in English-language poetry in the early decades of this century. More recently, Robert Bly insisted that American writers attend to the Spanish and South American poets of the "deep image" in order to open themselves to the less-tamed realms of imagination. Each successfully altered the literary practice of his contemporaries. William Tyndale, who also translated in the spirit of correction, offers a more cautionary example. Hoping to bring greater accuracy to the scriptures in English, he published the first Biblical translation made from earlier Hebrew and Greek texts rather than from the then-standard Latin—and was burned at the stake in 1536. His Catholic accusers found too Protestant a cast in his "untrue translations."

For me, the decision to enter into the realm of translation came about through the meeting of accidental opportunity and long-standing desire, under circumstances I will relate a little later. I have translated as an amateur, almost always in collaboration, and always because there was something I had encountered in a brief sampling and wanted to read more fully. I have translated, then, for perhaps the most selfish of motives: simple greed. There were poems I wanted to read, but they lived in another tongue.

ONCE the process of translation begins, the translator enters into an erotic engagement with the chosen text, reading the poem again and again for its meaning, its resonance, its kinetic and musical bodies, its ambiguities, rhetoric, grammar, images, and tropes—for all the rustling of its many leaves and for the silences at its roots as well. The translator reads in the desire to join with what she reads, placing the life of the poem thoroughly within her own, discovering how each entering word modifies that life. As with any engagement, there are the families to consider as well: the translator's knowledge of the historical and cultural context of a poem, its religious background and its intentions, and the translator's own development as poet and as person—all these will contribute to the outcome.

In the midst of this interchange, both translator and poem change their natures. The poem that in its original form may contain a multitude of possible readings becomes in translation a poem in which a particular interpretation is more likely to predominate—though if the translation is a good one, the new poem will also have its resonance and overtones, its unconsciously preserved wisdom. The translator is changed in the way any important encounter changes a person: taking in a new vision of being, our own grows to include it. Eventually, the efforts and pleasures of courtship come to their natural conclusion—there is the leap, the moment of union when the translator joins with a poem so intimately that there is no longer a sense of "self" and "other," and the poem emerges, as if for the first time, within one's own heart and tongue.

At times in this process, the translator may feel not only a union of self with poem, but also a kind of identity with the translated author. Paul Valéry describes this sense of merging well in his essay in *The Art of Poetry* on translating Virgil, "Variations on the 'Eclogues'":

> Faced with my Virgil, I had the sensation (well known to me) of a poet at work. From time to time I argued absently with myself about this

famous book, set in its millennial fame, with as much freedom as if it had been a poem of my own on the table before me. At moments, I caught myself wanting to change something in the venerable text. . . . "Why not?" I said to myself, returning from this short absence. Why not?   *(trans. Denise Folliot)*

Freedom from the words of the original combined with a deep love of its words lies at the heart of translation. In the act of true translation, as opposed to the act of parsing out meaning, there is a moment when all prior knowledge of a poem dissolves, when the words that *were* are shed as a snake sheds its skin and the words that *are* take on their own life. Some part of the poem's essential life, its way of traveling through the world, must pass through the emptiness that runs like a broad river-gorge between languages: the impossibility of any word, even the simplest, remaining the same in a different tongue. Think of *bread, panne, brot*—their entirely different flavors.

Translation occurs precisely in that moment of forgetfulness and dissolving, when everything already comprehended through great effort—grammar, vocabulary, meaning, background—falls away. In that surrendering instant, the translator turns from the known shore of the original to look into that emptiness where the outlines of the new poem begin to resolve, a changed landscape appearing through mist. This experience, as Valéry wrote, is almost indistinguishable from the experience of writing itself: the sense of active creative discovery is the same. Yet somehow, the original ur-poem is also there, crossing along with the translator the waters that surge between Rilke's Unsayable source and words.

▾   ▾   ▾   ▾   ▾

I F   A   C E R T A I N sense of freedom is essential to translation, that is because fidelity's claims are so strong. Yet fidelity is in this realm a chimera. A literal word-for-word trot is not a translation. The attempt to recreate qualities of sound is not a translation. The simple conveyance of meaning is not a translation. What then can fidelity— even a fidelity already recognized as failure—mean?

Every translator can offer principles and explanations for having been more or less literal at this point, choosing one nuance of meaning over another at that, omitting "the untranslatable" here or adding there some information commonly understood within a poem's home culture. In my experience, though, these are after-the-fact descriptions of a process of choice-making as mysterious and intuitive as writing itself. Fidelity's multifaceted nature, impossible to define in the abstract, reveals itself only in practice. The attentiveness and flexibility required are as individual as those that make for a good marriage.

Writers and critics have nonetheless long debated the nature of translation, its possibilities, philosophies, and practice. Samuel Johnson, for instance, offered the oft-quoted opinion that the true test of a translation is whether it makes a good poem in English—a statement that holds myriad assumptions within its scope. Robert Frost, however, made clear that for him the original music was all—and unreproducible—in his famous assertion that "the poetry is what gets lost in translation." But "the poetry is what gets transformed" is Octavio Paz's response to Frost:

> After all, poetry is not merely the text. The text produces the poem: a set of sensations and meanings. . . . With different means, but playing a similar role, you can produce similar results. I say similar, but not identical: translation is an art of analogy, the art of finding correspondences. An art of shadows and echoes . . . of producing, with a different text, a poem similar to the original.

Most poets who translate share Paz's sense of the process, though the ways they interpret it vary. The quest to reproduce the original poem's effects as much as its words—an idea Valéry also expressed—

permits the issue of "fidelity" and "license" to dissolve on the tongue. Only such an understanding allows the impossible work to go on at all.

Walter Benjamin, in the classic essay "The Task of the Translator," raises the issue of another kind of fidelity. Benjamin suggests that a poem should not read entirely as though it were written in the new language but should preserve some flavor of the syntax and grammar of the original. To convey this idea, Benjamin quotes Rudolf Pannwitz:

> Our translations, even the best ones, proceed from a wrong premise. They want to turn Hindi, Greek, English, into German, instead of turning German into Hindi, Greek, or English. . . . The basic error of the translator is that he preserves the state in which his own language happens to be instead of allowing his language to be powerfully affected by the foreign tongue. . . . He must go back to the primal elements of language itself and penetrate to the point where work, image, and tone converge. He must expand and deepen his language by means of the foreign language. It is not generally realized to what extent this is possible.

The proposal intrigues. Robert Fitzgerald, however, has responded to it by saying: "To make something that is strange to our ears would not be doing justice to the work that was not strange to theirs." Fitzgerald's fidelity is to the work as it affects us, Pannwitz's to the various nature of thought in different languages. Each practice brings its gifts, though my own inclination is closer to Fitzgerald's: to seek an English-language style that reflects the language qualities of the specific work rather than those of the home language as a whole.

ALMOST all translators face the question of whether or how to retain a poem's formal structure. The main philosophies closely mirror those we have just seen: some translators attempt to replicate the formal qualities of the original, others try instead to convey the underlying effect without reference to prosodic form. The fundamental issue is not merely if form should be translated, but whether it can be.

It is worth remembering that in formal poems, as much as free verse, the subtle parts are where the real musical power is likely to lie. Occasionally, both form and content can flourish in the new version; Richard Wilbur's translations from the French are examples of what is possible when a poet, linguist, and translator of genius hold one pen. But in lesser hands, a coarsely mechanical reproduction of outer form can be more a disservice to a work's nature than the decision to turn to free verse. Form ill-married to meaning and breath places over the translated words a badly painted mask, a parody of their original grace.

Yet free-verse translation may seem a kind of surrender. Still, what is lost in that choice can be remedied at least a little with information about the original's form. Once the reader knows a poem was originally in rhymed couplets, those effects can be intuited; it is less easy to guess what else has been altered in order to reproduce rhyme-scheme and meter in a poorly done formal translation.

Best are bilingual editions, put into the Roman alphabet if necessary, along with a guide to pronunciation. Given this help, even a reader wholly ignorant of a language can sound a work out, while those with some familiarity can use the translation to gain better entry to the original, as well as to judge for themselves the choices that have been made. Still another method can be found in the many Penguin Books anthologies where the original appears accompanied only by a prose trot. If the reader is lucky, a work will exist in multiple translations—in their points of overlap and divergence, the hands of translators and author may be distinguished, though the original music remains out of reach.

Free-verse translation can still honor the essential movement of a poem. The parallelism of Chinese poetry is an indispensable and anchoring part of its nature, for example; though that language's tonal parallels cannot be brought into English, parallel sentence constructions can be kept. Their shapeliness holds part of the poem's information, subtly communicating its relationship to order, balance, and form itself.

To take another case, the alternating five and seven syllables of Japanese poetry are something most American ears fail to perceive, and so my own choice as a translator was to forego the original meter. But I held to the number of lines: to render a three-line haiku as a couplet, or a five-line *tanka* as a quatrain, for me would mask the asymmetrical unfolding of the originals, making them seem less different in aesthetic and worldview than they are. Yet many translators—from both ends of the spectrum of freedom and form—have chosen differently.

A translator's first obligation is to convey each poem's particular strengths. If music and intricacy of form are the greatest pleasures in the original, this is what the translator should try to capture; if a startling directness of language is at the heart of a work, then straightforwardness should govern the new version as well. Imagery, sensibility, feeling, sound, ideas—any of these can become the through-line of a poem's unfolding. One cannot perform vivisection on a living being; some mix of these elements will be present in any well-realized poem, and equally present in any translation. The issue, though, is to what extent a new version can mirror the original, to what extent it must find some differing path toward the same destination, "so that always, within each delight, / we gaze at what is purely single and joined."

Every great poet leaves the landscape of poetry altered by his or her passage through it. One way this alteration occurs is when a writer comes to a new mode of vision through either making or reading translations; Whitman's *Leaves of Grass,* with its King James Bible-influenced rhythms and lists, is a good example of that process. The strengths of a great poem or tradition are only truly *translated* if they come into the language in a way that can then be used. Just as English takes in foreign words (*tao, zeitgeist, anima*) when no native one will do, so forms of poetic thought discovered in translation can work to expand what may be said.

"Unless there is a new mind, there cannot be a new line," William Carlos Williams wrote. The converse is true as well. When there *is* a new mind, or a new line, American poetry has shown a spongelike ability to absorb it. The imagist movement, of which Williams was part, brought to American poets some of the strategies of classical Chinese and Japanese poetry. A more recent example is the adoption of the *ghazal.* An Urdu form consisting of long-lined couplets linked in the original primarily by sound, it ends with a "signature" couplet in which the poet includes his or her name. In 1970, a scholar of Urdu, Aijaz Ahmad, invited seven American poets to help translate a collection of ghazals by the poet Ghalib. Some were translators as well as poets, others not. Several went on to use the form in their own writing; Adrienne Rich in particular included a number of haunting ghazals in her subsequent collections. From that beginning, the ghazal has entered contemporary poetry as a mode of writing marked more by a disconnectedness between thoughts and stanzas than by the intricate prosodic rules of the original form. But this oblique adoption is precisely how translation transforms: not by exact imitation but through a kind of hybridization, in which some kernel of the original's power is both preserved and changed.

Translation is one way poetic mind refreshes itself, old forms of thought-making opening themselves to new ones. It is also a way the old is itself made new: one side-effect of translation (unless the work is also contemporary) is the recasting of a poem's relationship to time.

This happens because translations are virtually always placed into the language of the present.

When an original grows old, its dated words and syntax serve as a kind of watermark. Age in itself gives substance—what has lasted becomes a thing worth keeping. An older poem's increasing strangeness of language is part of its beauty, in the same way that the cracks and darkening of an old painting become part of its luminosity in the viewer's mind: they enter not only the physical painting, but our vision of it as well. This is why seeing an old painting suddenly "restored" can be unnerving—we recognize a tampering with its relationship to time, miss the scented smoke of the centuries' passage. For just this reason, seminal works such as Chaucer's *Canterbury Tales* in English or *The Tale of Genji* in Japanese are "translated" from archaic into contemporary language only when they have become almost unintelligible to general readers (and even then, students continue to memorize a passage or two in the original form). But in bringing a work from one language into another, translators must decide whether to attempt to instill in their work a false patina of age or to recreate the freshness of diction the piece would have had in its own time. Usually, the second approach is chosen.

Older translations can become works of interest in their own right. People turn to Pope's Homer not to know Homer, but to know Pope's vision of him; most who now read Chapman's version have been sent there by Keats. Pound's versions of Rihaku (Li Po), called the best existing translation from the Chinese when they were made, are still thought that by some; they are also thoroughly Pound's. In his work we can see the American poet—thoroughly the product of his own time and tradition—suffusing and being suffused by the Chinese. The translations mark the tangible joining of two great tributaries of poetry's river.

For the most part, though, translations are ephemeral: each time current diction changes or the culture's idea of what constitutes a poem shifts, new translations are made. Victorian-era translators of Japanese haiku commonly put the unrhymed originals into rhyme—a poetry without rhyme was not, for many of these scholar-translators, poetry at all. We can see how such older translations reflect the aesthetic expectations of their makers in unconscious as well as conscious ways, yet it is virtually impossible to see the biases of one's own age. The continual remaking of translations may seem like a movement further and further from the original; it can be seen also as a way of returning a work to the perennial freshness of its original state.

As George Steiner has pointed out, the practice of choosing archaic language when translating ancient texts, while now rare, can serve a useful purpose, helping to ground the new version within the linguistic history of its new culture. A reader encountering a style of language he had come to expect in literature from the past would feel immediately and strongly "at home" in the new work, particularly if the work in question was already part of his cultural tradition. The King James Bible, surely the greatest translation English has seen, was put into a diction several generations older than that spoken at the time it was made. Creative accident, rather than conscious decision, may have played a part in this—the King James translators had been instructed to retain the best of earlier versions. But however it happened, the result was a translation whose clarity, beauty, and power so overwhelm that its language forms remain, four centuries later, a living force.

▼   ▼   ▼   ▼   ▼

M Y OWN experience as a translator dates from 1985, when during a year as a Guggenheim fellow I started collaborating with Mariko Aratani on a translation of the poetry of Ono no Komachi and Izumi Shikibu, the two foremost women poets of Japan's classical period. I had first encountered a handful of their tanka in English as an undergraduate taking courses in Japanese literature in translation. The Japanese women's concerns—love and transience—paralleled my own, and despite the passage of a millennium since its composition, their poetry held for me an immediacy and power that was life-altering. Not only did it affect my own writing, it led me three years later to undertake the study of Buddhism; in 1979 I was lay-ordained in the lineage of Sōtō Zen.

I first realized the need for a larger selection of Komachi's work in 1971, and I waited almost fifteen years for someone to make it possible for me to read more. Then a fortunate introduction to Mariko—a weaver, jazz pianist, and native speaker of Japanese who also loved the classical-period poets—led to our translating a dozen poems together for a journal. We quickly decided to continue working toward a book-length selection of the two poets' work, eventually titled *The Ink Dark Moon*. Although in this account I will say "I" in describing the way a few poems from that book traveled from literal to final versions, Mariko Aratani's contribution at every stage was indispensible to the finished work. Her expertise went far beyond skills of language.

The poems appear here first as they did on the worksheet Mariko and I devised. During weekly meetings over the course of a year, we created such a sheet for each poem we considered for the book. Along with the original and rough translations were Mariko's comments covering background information, grammatical uncertainties, the nuances of certain words, and so on. I wrote down each Japanese poem in *romaji* (the Roman alphabet transliteration of spoken Japanese). The core English meaning (or meanings, if more than one were possible) appeared below each corresponding word, and the metrical line-units of the Japanese were separated by a slash mark. Through this system Mariko could give me access to both the sound of the original poem and its original syntax, something that even the most literal rough translation cannot do. I would then take the sheets away and work toward finished translations, returning them always to her for rechecking.

Here is a first poem, relatively straightforward to translate, by Izumi Shikibu, the greatest of Japan's women poets:

NADOTE KIMI / MUNASHIKI SORA NI / KIENIKEMU /
why   you   empty   sky   in   disappear did(?)

AWAYUKI DANI MO / FUREBA   FURU YO NI
Frail snow even   !   when falling falling world in

A prose headnote—not uncommon in Japanese poetry—offers more information about the poem's background: "Around the time Naishi [Shikibu's daughter] died, snow fell, then melted away."

Why did you vanish
into empty sky?
Even the fragile snow,
when it falls,
falls in this world.

The finished translation is quite close to the literal, with only minor adjustments of word order and a few changes of word choice: "vanish" for "disappear," "fragile" for "frail." Japanese does not use articles before nouns, and so in bringing the poem into English, I might have also chosen to say "Why did you vanish / into *the* empty sky?" Why didn't I? One reason was rhythmic—the extra syllable seemed to my ear to clutter the poem. But more important, there was the difference in meaning. Without the article, Shikibu's daughter not only rises amid her cremation smoke into the sky, she also becomes that emptiness and absence—an effect that the inclusion of the article *the* would have diluted.

The five-line free-verse translation reflects but is not identical to the formal structure of the original. Japanese poetry's conventions for transcription onto the page are unlike those of English. Its vertical columns do not use visual breaks to mark each metrical unit, and at least one translator from the Japanese, Hiroaki Sato, advocates forgoing them entirely. My own feeling, however, is that for Western readers the line break is the fundamental signal that they are encountering a poem: words to be met with the mind and expectations of poetry. Even had I followed strictly the Japanese tanka's syllabic pattern of 5-7-5-7-7, the translation's fundamental "poem-ness" would not have been clear to American readers: English verse speaks a language of stresses rather than count, and American ears do not hear the pattern. Further, the two languages differ enough that metrically exact translations often are forced either to leave out parts of a poem's meaning or else add unnecessary words to fill the count. Both reasons affected my choice of form.

Another poem, one of Shikibu's most famous, required more extensive changes to bring the Japanese into English:

KUROKAMI NO / MIDARE   MO   SHIRAZU /
Black hair   's   messiness, tangling (obj)   without knowing
                                                     without caring

UCHIFUSEBA / MAZU   KAKIYARISHI /
when lying prone   first   stroked
                   clear

HITO   ZO   KOISHIKI
person ! longing

This poem is one continuous sentence, and the first task in approaching it is to determine the grammatical clauses governing meaning. In Japanese, word order is often the reverse of that in

English and a syntactical break often appears after the first two or three line-units in a tanka. Using these principles, the poem's basic meaning quickly resolves itself: "While lying down without caring about black hair's tangling, longing for the person who stroked it first." This then became:

Lying alone,
my black hair tangled,
uncombed,
I long for the one
who touched it first.

The largest change between the original and the translation is that the poem has been placed into a grammatical voice, the first person. Many tanka, like this one, do not specify their speaker or point of view. This reflects not only Japanese grammar but also a culture in which experience itself, not the subjective frame around it, is felt to be important; a few lightly sketched phrases evoke a situation in which the reader becomes an equal participant. English, however, demands grounding. To follow the original grammar too closely would only mute the impact and emotional immediacy the poem carries in its own language.

A second departure from the literal is the word *alone*. My after-the-fact explanation (in actual practice, this is simply how the poem spoke itself after the studying, joining, and forgetting earlier described) is that it rises out of *shirazu*—"without knowing or caring." This woman neglecting her hair is surely in the solitary aftermath of a love affair. Finding herself alone, she has no reason now to attend to her physical beauty; but she remembers such a time—not the recent love, but her first.

Shikibu, we know, was disowned by her family and divorced by her husband (Naishi's father) after she began a love affair with an imperial prince, who soon died. Later in life she took many lovers, and the reputation of "floating woman" came to accompany her reputation as a poet of surpassing insight and lyrical skill. Shikibu apparently tried to reestablish communication with her husband many times; though he never replied to her letters, he is almost certainly the early love she recalls in this poem.

A last change from the literal is that for the one word *midare* I used two: "tangled, uncombed." "Uncombed" and the earlier "alone" probably arose together, the near-rhyme giving the poem a music satisfying to my ear and the sound of the long *o* holding the poem's resonant grief; the word also reflects the indifference to self contained in *shirazu*, "without caring." The textured physicality of the word works as well to bring Shikibu's presence vividly into the poem. This is true to the original's spirit: Japanese critics have long pointed out that Shikibu's tangled black hair is one of very few references to the details of physical life in all Japanese poetry.

I took more liberty still with this poem by Ono no Komachi, written around the year 850:

ITO SEMETE / KOISHIKI TOKI WA /
very extremely longing time —

UBATAMA NO / YORU NO KOROMO O /
hiougi 's night 's clothing (obj)
nut

KAESHITE ZO KIRU
turned ! wear
inside
out

Born roughly one hundred fifty years before Shikibu, Komachi was one of the first women members of the court culture to benefit from a newly developed system for transcribing spoken Japanese using Chinese characters. During this period Chinese served the Japanese court as the language of both writing and government, much as Latin functioned as the learned language of medieval Europe. Education in Chinese was reserved for men, however, so only with this new writing system could women participate fully in the literary life of a culture in which artistic skill was becoming a paramount value, and the exchange of poetry a central mode of communication.

Poems were written to express private feeling, but also to conduct a courtship, convey condolences, or demonstrate publicly (in frequently held official competitions) one's talent, learning, and refined sensibilities. Because the imperial court's women, unlike the men, wrote solely in the vernacular, they became primary creators of the great literary flowering of that age. Komachi in particular, living at the start of the era, brought to the writing of tanka a fiercely passionate nature, technical mastery as a poet, and, at times, a profound insight into Buddhist teachings.

The poem above shows Komachi's explicit revelation of passion. It also makes use of a technical device specific to Japanese poetry, the *makurakotoba*, or pillow word. A pillow word, much like a Homeric epithet, is an image that regularly accompanies its noun—the *wine-dark* sea is one familiar Homeric example. Like the cushion on which the round bowl of a temple bell is placed, a pillow word worked both to elevate a poem and to increase its resonance. And as with the wine-dark sea, the meaning of pillow words are often so archaic as to be baffling, unless one somehow discovers that the ancient Greeks did in fact make a wine whose color was closer to purple-blue than red.

The poem shows Komachi alone and missing an unnamed lover. Many of her poems are responses to seeing her absent lover in a dream. In one, she wishes she had never wakened; in another, she determines to commit herself to a life of dreaming; in a third, she mourns the cruel fact that even in their dream-meetings she and her beloved meet in the fear of being seen. In this poem, however, we see

Komachi before sleep, turning her nightgown inside out—a folk custom believed to make one dream of one's love.

Here is the version appearing in *The Ink Dark Moon:*

> When my desire
> grows too fierce
> I wear my bedclothes
> inside out,
> dark as the night's rough husk.

To American ears, the opening phrase of the original might seem abstract rather than emotional, but the phrase *ito semete* ("very extremely") is rare in tanka and would have stood out; later in the poem, the word *zo* also functions as an intensifier. My response was to replace the usual translation of *koishiki*, "longing," with the stronger "fierce desire." Because Japanese readers would at least be aware of the folk custom explaining why one might reverse one's nightgown when feeling longing, I chose to begin the poem with "When," to indicate that a causal connection exists. I also tried to give my translation of the pillow word, "hiougi-nut," an extra imagistic vividness and weight. Researching this pillow word for "night," I learned that the nut has a virtually black shell; I then made rather free with the image to create the last line of my version.

One thing translation teaches is that other choices may always be made. Here is an alternative translation of mine, closer to the original in one way, more free in another:

> Longing,
> fiercely longing—
> To dream of him
> I turn my bedclothes inside out
> this dark-husked night.

For a final example of my own experience as a translator, here is another poem by Komachi. One of her most famous, it illustrates a different technical device of Japanese poetry, the *kakekotoba*, or pivot word: a word that can be read in two different ways, both intended to be part of the poem. (The pivot words below are indicated by an asterisk between the alternative meanings in English.)

HANO NO IRO WA / UTSURI NI KERI NA /
flower 's color (subj) faded has alas

ITAZURI NI / WAGA MI YO NI FURU /
uselessly my body world in aging
                              *
                              falling

NAGAME SESHI MA NI
long rains doing while
*
watching

Komachi here confronts transience in a manner quite different from that of Shikibu in her poem mourning her daughter. When she wrote these words, Komachi most likely was still in the midst of her life at court but would have been realizing that time must be nearing its end. A single woman would not be welcome in that world so centered on love and beauty once her own beauty was gone.

While watching
the long rains falling on this world,
my heart, too, fades
with the unseen color
of the spring flowers.

The heart of the poem is its complex and skilled interweaving of its various images of passing time. No translation can convey kakekotoba with justice, and it is possible that no one from a different culture can fully appreciate the depth of regret expressed in Komachi's image of uselessly fading spring flowers. Where a poet of ancient Rome responded to transience and mortality with the proud attitude of *carpe diem*, the poet of classical-era Japan acquiesced with a heart full of sorrow, believing that such deep feeling was the mark of being human. The adjacent pivot words *furu* and *nagame*, with their multiple readings, create between themselves a kind of harmonic resonance. The poet is watching her own aging, the long rains are falling, she looks out of her window upon a rain that causes flowers to fade without being viewed, she herself grows older without being known by her lover. It is the other side of Komachi's passionate dream-life we see in this poem: the long hours of waking and solitude, the realization that human life is fleeting and the pleasures of youth and beauty even more fleeting.

Unlike most of the poems Mariko Aratani and I translated, this one exists in many different English versions; it was one of the poems that had first aroused my interest in Komachi and her work. Because it is much translated, and well, I felt a certain freedom (and a certain responsibility) to make it my own. In this version—one of eight or ten quite different drafts that I made—the idea of "aging" is implied by the fading spring flowers rather than stated, "uselessly" is clarified for the Western reader with "unseen," and the word for "body" became "heart" in an effort to make a poetic statement that flowed as seamlessly as possible. A "heart," I think, can both "watch" and "fade"; for a "body" to do so would seem incongruous. I could as easily have simply used the pronoun *I*, since the phrase *my body* is often used simply to indicate the grammatical first person. That is the choice made by Kenneth Rexroth, in his concise translation of this poem, and also by Burton Watson:

The colors of the flower fade
as the long rains fall,
as lost in thought,
I grow older.

(trans. Kenneth Rexroth)

The beauty of the flowers faded—
no one cared—
and I watched myself
grow old in the world
as the long rains were falling.

(trans. Burton Watson)

From even this small sampling, it is easy to see the range of possible choices in bringing these thirty-one syllables into English. In yet another version, Rexroth allowed himself almost complete freedom:

As certain as color
Passes from the petal,
Irrevocable as flesh,
The gazing eye falls through the world.

(trans. Kenneth Rexroth)

Though Japanese tanka are unrhymed, the varying sound of the words is part of their effect—much as it is in American free verse—and I would not want to close my description of working with these poems without touching on that part of the task. In my own version of Komachi's poem, the consonants and vowels shift as it progresses, culminating in the final "flowers," which contains most of the recurring sound elements of the poem; as in the opening line, especially, of the Japanese, the sounds of *o* and *a* preside. Japanese and English prosody are quite different, but my hope was that at least some of the effects of Komachi's music had found its way into the translation.

▼   ▼   ▼   ▼   ▼

TRANSLATION is one way of learning what delicate clockwork causes a poem to keep accurate faith with music, meaning, and time. But even beyond this, translated poetry brings new realms of being. For me, encountering Komachi's and Shikibu's poetry at the age of eighteen wasn't simply an introduction to new ways of making poems that were moving and beautiful—their work taught me to see and feel differently, introduced to my life a new vocabulary of responses.

The twentieth century's flowering of translation brings with it the richness good poetry always brings: new spiritual and emotional and ethical understandings, new ways of seeing, new tools of knowledge as significant for an increase of inner life as radio telescopes are for an increased knowledge of the spiraling arms of distant space. If translators have an overriding responsibility, it is to carry these new powers in English as fully as possible, by understanding what may serve as a means of perception, what must remain in the ground of the original language, untranslatable and beyond reach. Our desire as readers remains the same as that expressed by the translators of the King James Bible—to break open the shell, that we may eat the kernel.

Translation that serves truly will widen our knowledge of what poetry—what humanness—is. When I read, as one still can, some spirited defense of English iambic meter as a basic expression of human nature, I despair. How can the authors of such essays not acknowledge that great literatures have been made of other meters than our binary or triple ones? That not all languages are stressed? That English-language forms, though they may be full of strengths and powers to our ears, are not the only possible forms? We should know these things not to reject the powers of our own linguistic history, but to welcome the powers of others. Poetry's task is to increase the available stock of reality, R. P. Blackmur said. It does this by reflecting for us our many human faces, our animal faces, our face of insect wings, our face of ocean and cliff. The world is large and, like Caliban's island, full of noises; a true poem reflects this, whether in the original or in translation. To try to encompass such knowledge, to be willing to fail, to prepare as fully as possible for the work of poetry, to make the attempt in the recognition that any understanding is one among many—this is all we can do, as translators or as readers.

Many writers describe the attempt to bring the world into language as itself an act of translation. It is an attempt that must always fall short, and still the effort is made. One depiction of why appears in the inner dialogue captured in Robinson Jeffers's sonnet "Love the Wild Swan." The sonnet progresses by straightforward rhyme until the final three lines, which move into eye-rhymes that are not ear-rhymes. Then the poem, like the wild swan it describes, begins to escape our human forms, though not our lives.

Love the Wild Swan

"I hate my verses, every line, every word.
Oh pale and brittle pencils ever to try
One grass-blade's curve, or the throat of one bird
That clings to twig, ruffled against white sky.
Oh cracked and twilight mirrors ever to catch
One color, one glinting flash, of the splendor of things.
Unlucky hunter, Oh bullets of wax,
The lion beauty, the wild-swan wings, the storm of the wings."
—This wild swan of a world is no hunter's game.
Better bullets than yours would miss the white breast,
Better mirrors than yours would crack in the flame.
Does it matter whether you hate your . . . self? At least
Love your eyes that can see, your mind that can
Hear the music, the thunder of the wings. Love the wild swan.

This last, brief poem is by the ninth-century poet Kūkai—the Japanese Buddhist monk who, according to legend, developed the system for using Chinese characters to write Japanese words. Like the poem by Rilke at this chapter's beginning, it describes the relationship of source and manifestation; of word and Mind and the manifest, multiple world.

Singing Image of Fire

A hand moves, and the fire's whirling takes different shapes,
Triangles, squares: all things change when we do.
The first word, "Ah," blossomed into all others.
Each of them is true.

The Myriad Leaves of Words

▾ ▾ ▾ ▾ ▾ ▾ ▾ ▾ ▾ ▾

In 905, the poet Ki no Tsurayuki took up his brush to compose the earliest exploration of poetry's nature in Japanese literature. "The poetry of Japan," he wrote in his preface to the *Kokinshū*, first of a series of imperially commissioned anthologies,

has its seeds in the human heart and mind and grows into the myriad leaves of words. Because people experience many different phenomena in this world, they express that which they think and feel in their hearts in terms of all they see and hear. A nightingale singing among the blossoms, the voice of a pond-dwelling frog—listening to these, what living being would not respond with his own poem? It is poetry that effortlessly moves the heavens and the earth, awakens the world of invisible spirits to deep feeling, softens the relationship between men and women, and consoles the hearts of fierce warriors.

(trans. Jane Hirshfield and Mariko Aratani)

Japanese poetry has its seeds in the human heart and mind and grows into the myriad leaves of words—it is easy to skim the words lightly. Yes, we think, poetry comes out of emotional and intellectual experience, everyone knows that; and we notice also, perhaps, that the idea arrives within a pretty metaphor of seed and leaf. Yet looked at more closely, these few words unfold one of the core strategies of Japanese literature: the interpenetration of natural and human realms.

What would the sentence be without its image? Into what abstraction could we translate those myriad leaves of words? The image weaves a green canopy of meaning, simultaneously elusive and clear, finely detailed and sweeping. We catch the green scent of the thought, hear its slight rustle, glimpse the light sifting between its shadows; yet we cannot say in other words what this leafy language raises into comprehension.

"Words' leaves" was a common metaphor in Tsurayuki's time and place, Japan's Heian era, which began when the court moved to Heian-kyō (present-day Kyoto) in 794, and ended around 1185, when a long period of relative peace gave way to the Kamakura age of warring clans and samurai. The phrase is an old one, probably predating written literature. Here it appears in a ninth-century poem by Ono no Komachi, whom Tsurayuki honored as one of his collection's "six poetic geniuses":

> Truly now I've grown old
> in the winter rains.
> Even the words' leaves
> of love
> change in their falling.

The phrase—*koto no ha*—thoroughly entangles our human tongue with nature's. It creates a permeability and a sympathy, and through its gate, feeling, time, and mystery all may enter.

How does the image achieve this? Tsurayuki goes on to say: *Because people experience many different phenomena in this world, they express that which they think and feel in their hearts in terms of all they see and hear.* Primordial experience is nameless and without form; still, we find our way into the life of expressive language by means of an inner attention tuned to the outer world's voice. Images, metaphors, similes, and stories are sliding doors, places of opening through which subjective and objective may penetrate and become each other. When the words of Komachi's lover enter the late autumn leaves, they grow dry and insubstantial—the outer shape of his affection may appear unchanged, but now it is brittle and weightless, its green brightness extinguished. The trope is no decorative addition, but a fundamental tool for the seeding of meaning: by a fertile, imaginative turning of outer image, we plow the ground of our lives. Japanese poetry keeps close to this primary mode of conceptualization—it uses the power held in the seen, the heard, the tasted, to quicken and instruct and unfold.

Tsurayuki continues, *A nightingale singing among the blossoms, the voice of a pond-dwelling frog—listening to these, what living being would not respond with his own poem?* This sentence develops still further the idea of interpenetration between human and nonhuman realms, describing how poetry moves, moment by moment, in both directions. The world's effortless expression reaches outward and summons the only answer we have for its various music—a human song, a poem. The voice of the natural and the voice of the poet meet, Tsurayuki says, in an irresistible duet; we are as helpless to refuse the exchange as is one owl hearing the call of another across the woods. And the unspoken name for this joining might be eros—for why do nightingales sing, or frogs, if not for love?

And what of the activities of poetry? Tsurayuki writes that it moves the large realms of heaven and earth, awakens supernatural spirits to the feelings of people, and, wholly in the human realm, tempers sorrow, anger, and the tumultuous course of desire. From high to low, from the most impersonal to the most intimate, there is no part of existence poetry fails to touch. And the range of effect Tsurayuki finds in poetry as a whole is mirrored in individual works: in poem after poem, the concerns of the passionate heart flow seamlessly into those of metaphysics and spirit. What links them in any particular tanka, more often than not, is the recognition of transience—a fact of existence that cuts across every moment of human perception, every activity of body, mind, and heart.

▾   ▾   ▾   ▾   ▾

IT IS impossible to understand Japanese poetry without knowing something of the Buddhist and Shinto culture from which it springs. Shinto's ethos of omnipresent, indwelling spirits underlies every natural image. The *kami,* or gods, of Shinto belief inhabit not only the mountain passes of the actual countryside but also those of the poems—each bent pine tree, seaweed-filled bay, even wind, is charged with an abiding and informing presence of its own. Japan's earliest literary works, mythological accounts of the country's origins that link the imperial family to the age of the gods, are almost purely Shinto in feeling. But by the eighth century, Japanese poetry had become soaked through with a deeply Buddhist sensibility as well.

The first quality most Westerners think of when considering Japanese poetry is its extraordinary brevity. Various form-related explanations for this have been put forward, but none makes clear why a meter of five and seven alternating beats should be any less viable for sustaining a long poem than, say, the blank verse of Milton's *Paradise Lost.* A more intriguing explanation emerges when we notice that extreme economy of poetic language appears in Japanese literature just as Buddhism and its worldview of impermanence also arrive. Five lines, thirty-one syllables: the tanka, from the seventh century to the seventeenth virtually the only form of serious expression in Japanese poetry. And then, in an even more severe compression, the haiku enters, a mere seventeen syllables with which to catch a world. But how long does each perception of the passing moment last? a single breath's intake? less?

Many Buddhist texts instruct that life is composed solely of fleeting instants. In the briefest of moments our first breath begins, our last ends. In the briefest of moments anger rises, or desire starts to wane. Japanese poetry distills itself from this present-moment awareness—a memory released in the faint scent of orange blossoms, the insight wakened by the silhouette of a crow on a branch at dusk. When we are most intensely alive—startled into alertness by love or pain or fear—we perceive with an added acuteness too often either forgotten or lost to distraction. But as the walls of monastic enclosure work to create focused attention, Japanese poetry's brevity similarly invites renewed intensity of perception. The brief poem murmurs, "Just this, just this," opening the reader to the sharpness of each blade of grass, on whose sword-tip the universe flowers.

"JUST this." Japanese poetry brings the concreteness of life first into view, and then into meaning's fragrance. The poems' brevity reminds us of the nature of time and our relationship to it, but their strong roots in the particular clarify that our fleeting lives do not simply "happen" and vanish, they *take place*—take place in the physical world; take place in the current of lived events; take place within a consciousness of interconnected being that is deeply Buddhist and within a sense of permeating aliveness fundamentally Shinto. The Greek poet Cavafy described the way poetry's consciousness transforms objects. Addressing the houses, cafés, and streets of which he has written for decades, he wrote, "For me, the whole of you has been transformed into feeling." The phrase holds the same knowledge Bashō points toward when he says in one haiku:

Hearing the cuckoo,
even in Kyoto
I long for Kyoto.

When particularity and emotion join in poetry, our sense of existence extends: the language of outward attention takes what is present and makes it a thing more knowable, clarified, sheered. It is not any moment, but this very moment, that a Japanese poem contemplates and preserves; not any feeling, but the one emotion pressed like wine from its underlying events. And there are underlying events—behind almost every tanka stands the essence of a particular story, a set of circumstances. Even poems written in response to an assigned topic at a competition were framed as specific moments, grounded in situation and time.

Haiku are a bit different: often less personal in their compass, an underlying narrative or context may be less easy to intuit. Though often such stories are there, if difficult for a person from a different culture to recognize, there are also many haiku whose attention turns elsewhere than personal life. Here is one such poem, again by Bashō:

Stillness—
soaking into the rocks,
the cicada's cries.

Seemingly a moment of pure perception, this poem also portrays a state of being. Though the poem is rooted in an actual visit to a mountain temple, a prose notation written by Bashō tells us his intention—to present the condition of "profound quietness, the heart-mind open and transparent." ("Heart-mind" is a concept English lacks, but in Japanese the one word *shin* includes both the realm of mind and that of the feeling heart.) Bashō's subject is one independent of place and time, of the stories and plot lines of self. But even the condition of transparence realizes itself within the stitched fabric of the phenomenal world, and all good haiku are precise in their seeing, true to the facts of the outer. Neither the universal nor the personal can be pointed at in any other way. "To generalize," as Blake irascibly reminds us in his scribbled marginalia, "is to be an Idiot. To Particularize is the alone distinction of merit."

SEVENTEEN or even thirty-one syllables pass quickly, and Japanese literary convention offers numerous ways to make explicit the particularity behind poems. Many tanka have introductory headnotes, a prose sentence or two explaining the circumstances of their composition. Further, several different forms exist in which poetry and prose intermingle. The *nikki*, a type of diary at times closer to fiction than to our conception of a private journal, can contain poetry as well as prose. The pillow book is another, less narrative kind of journal in which observations might be recorded in either prose or verse. In the realm of haiku there is the *haibun*, a brief unit of prose ending in a poem, and the *renga*, a form in which a series of poems by different authors are linked together, ringing changes upon one another's imagery and subjects. The classical-period tales called *monogatori*— the best known of these "novels" is *The Tale of Genji*, written by Murasaki Shikibu around the year 1000—can include hundreds of poems, some working to heighten emotion, others appearing as written or spoken communications between characters. In each of these hybrid forms, the poems flow directly from the circumstances of their narrative context; one could say with equal validity, though, that the narrative exists to prepare the reader for the poems' condensed precipitates of consciousness, circumstance, and time.

Particularity also enters Japanese poetry in the form of the *kigo*, the season-indicating word that every haiku contains. Sometimes these words are obvious in translation—"winter dawn," "autumn twilight." Other times the reader must recognize that certain birds or insects point to a specific time of year—the cricket to autumn, for example.

The *kigo* brings into a haiku both the concrete here-and-now and also awareness of passing time. Passing, because seasons exist only by differentiation: to contemplate the particular blossoms and winds and beings by which we know autumn or winter, summer or spring, is to remember that each exists within continual change.

A passage about this two-fold effect occurs in the *Kadenshō*, a treatise on the training of Nō actors written in the fifteenth century by Zeami, the foremost Japanese classical dramatist. It discusses *hana*, or "flowering," Zeami's name for an ineffable quality that only the greatest actors develop:

> Since every variety of tree and plant comes into bloom in its own time in one of the four seasons, we prize the timeliness and rarity of the blooming of each. So, too, in Nō: our minds take as "interesting" that which we experience as a rare thing. Now what we call *hana* or "flowering," what we call "interesting," and what we call "rarity" are not three separate things but really one and the same. But all flowers eventually are scattered; none stays in bloom. And it is precisely because it blooms and perishes that a flower holds our interest as something rare. So also in Nō: to know the flowering is first of all to know that nothing abides. *(trans. William LaFleur)*

Wallace Stevens framed the thought in more Western terms: "Death is the mother of Beauty."

Beauty and feeling matter in these poems. I have described Japanese poems as precipitates of their authors' lives. It is an odd word, yet I think true to the sense of a culture in which the practice of the arts and the conduct of daily life were intimately, inseparably entwined. The writing of poetry was not an activity only a few people might find of interest, but a core part of being human: for members of the Heian court culture, poetry was a primary means both of communication and of self-cultivation, practiced in solitude and in virtually every kind of social interchange.

Letters of condolence, get-well notes, government demotions, a request to borrow a book—all might be undertaken by means of composing and sending a tanka. Affairs of the heart were conducted almost entirely through the exchange of poems—courtships invited and ended; each erotic encounter completed only after the messenger page had finished his early-morning travels. And in private, writing served as a way to think and feel through one's life for oneself: no significant experience was felt to be entire until it had found expression in verse. Just as a cloud with sufficient water content will rain, a human heart with sufficient feeling would, in the ancient court of Japan, find its most natural expression in the words and music of poetry.

Capacity for deep feeling was among the most valued qualities of character in Heian-kyō. Such feeling, as Blake's words indicate, is not the product of general thought, but of real events, acutely seen, lived through with awareness. The transformation of the heart-mind's seed into the leaves of words both marks the presence of this awareness and requires a sharpened vision and sensibility before it can happen. Certain Zen traditions ask that any experience of Buddhist awakening be sealed with a four-line poem in whose words the teacher can know the student's ripeness of understanding. The writing of such a poem is not a statement about the experience, but part of the transformative moment itself; not the mirror of an event, but its natural completion. Similarly, for the Heian poet, poetry was a part of life itself, equal in standing to any other.

THE USE of description of the natural world to explore human feeling is a basic attribute of Japanese poetry. Though the device is found in all lyric poetries, it is absolutely central to this one. It appears clearly in these three poems by Ono no Komachi, who stands at the beginning of the tradition of the personal lyric in Japanese literature in much the same way that Sappho does in the West:

I thought those white clouds
were gathered
around some distant peak,
but already
they have risen between us.

It seems a time has come
when you've become like those horses
wild with spring
who long for distant fields
where the light mists rise.

This pine tree by the rock
must have its memories, too—
after a thousand years,
see how its branches
lean toward the ground.

In each of these tanka, the poet has found in nature what T. S. Eliot called the "objective correlative" of subjective experience. The suddenness with which seemingly distant clouds can rise between the poet and the person of whom she thinks is an image deeply particular, both visual and tactile. I read this poem always with a small shiver, one deepened perhaps by many afternoons of fog appearing suddenly over the coastal ridge on which I live. But for all its physical specificity, the description is at the same time evocative and open. Though Komachi's poem is traditionally believed to refer to a death, the words themselves transmit only the essence of her experience, carried on the few inked brushstrokes of her image. In this way the poem embodies another quality central to Japanese poetry, the complement of their particularity: suggestiveness.

The tendency of Japanese poems to focus more on inner states than on autobiographical detail may have its roots in the basic structures of language. English syntax demands that certain kinds of information be furnished. Japanese, however, though it can specify such things if necessary, often leaves open whether a noun is singular or plural, or a sentence spoken in the first, second, or third person. Verb tenses may similarly leave the time frame unclear. But in contrast to English, where such cues are relatively uncommon, Japanese makes use of a broad range of words to convey the emotional quality of an experience—intensifiers, emotive particles, and most well known, perhaps, the wonderfully flexible adjective *aware* (pronounced ah-wah-ray), whose meaning can range from "sad" to "delicious," depending on context. *Aware* is a signal as much as an expression of a specific meaning. One synonym might be *poignant*, but *poignant* is a word rarely used in everyday speech. *Aware* signifies the beauty of the fleeting world and also the presence of the human heart that feels it. The phrase *mono no aware*, "the sorrow of things," refers specifically to transience, but *aware* itself comes in a thousand different lights and shadings. It might be translated by a sigh as much as a word.

Japanese classical poetry successfully transcends barriers of time and language precisely because of the way it balances the precise and the suggestive, the specific and the unsaid. Outward-turning perceptions are grounded in the universal experience of the physical world; the meanings they carry, however, are left for readers to conjure within themselves. "This pine tree by the rock / must have its memories, too— / after a thousand years, / see how its branches / lean toward the ground"—the image is utterly precise. Yet each reader turns it toward private memories, because we are not told Komachi's. We may decide for ourselves to whom such a thought might have been offered, and why; decide if it represents a moment of inner contemplation, the murmured communication of a lover, or the comment of one close friend to another; or, since Komachi knew during her lifetime that her poetry had found public standing, we might think that the words of the poet are directed to us—in Emily Dickinson's phrase, a "letter to the world."

The weighted keel of the unspoken life under its words gives to Japanese poetry both accuracy and reserve. The experience of a poem is put forward, not the experiencer, and the poems do not coerce feeling, only invite it, by presenting the circumstances in which it may arise. It is this painterly quality, the use of outward presentation to hold inner meaning, that attracted the Imagist poets when they first read Japanese poems in translation at the start of the post-Romantic age. In tanka and haiku they discovered a tradition in which even the most passionate love poems lack self-display, as in these two poems by Izumi Shikibu, written around the turn of the last millennium:

> Those nights when we slept
> behind love's
> jeweled screen,
> were we even aware
> of the opening dawn skies?

> Remembering you ...
> The fireflies of this marsh
> seem like sparks
> that rise
> from my body's longing.

We are not shown what these lovers have done together, only its effect upon the author; still, the circumstances of the poems' composition is clear. Other tanka enlist the natural world to explore a situation left entirely unnamed, as in another poem of Shikibu's, stemming not from the realm of Eros but of Buddhist teaching. It holds the idea that enlightenment (for which the moon is a common symbol) cannot be attained unless we also make ourselves vulnerable to the experience of suffering. In paraphrase, the idea seems abstract—yet the poem is undidactic, sensual, and rich, trusting the image to do its own work:

Although the wind
blows terribly here,
the moonlight also leaks
between the roof planks
of this ruined house.

FOR classical-era poets, novelty of surface was unimportant; they sought to include and build on what had gone before rather than leave it behind. Some poems ring only the smallest changes upon earlier works, and many make use of well-known phrases, images, or place names precisely in order to bring older poems to mind. Such allusion allows the content of one poem to become part of another; it offers yet another device for expanding and making permeable the boundaries of a brief form.

A literature of allusion relies on its readers to share one body of knowledge, and even today, Japanese children play a game based on the memorization of an anthology of one hundred famous poems. Yet somehow, within this tradition of widely shared diction and imagery, each successful poem holds its own knowledge and flavor. This path of discovering the not-yet-expressed within the familiar recalls Gerard Manley Hopkins's perception of an abiding "dearest freshness deep down things." Japanese poetry—like the magnitude of being we find in love; like the mind of meditation, whether Buddhist or Christian; like the pressure of mortality on our lives—awakens us to the illimitable originality that resides in all being. Its concentrated resonance opens one path to that wellspring.

With the arrival first of renga and then the seventeenth-century haiku, the strictures of diction loosen. While images still draw for the most part on the natural world, less "poetic" subjects enter the poems—a ball of frozen sea slugs; lice, flies, and bedbugs; a stream of horse-piss next to a poet's sleeping head. Still, this opened frame of reference did not develop out of any deliberate intention to shock. Rather, it grew from the need for a refreshed verbal landscape, one closer to the actual experiences of writer and reader, who were no longer likely to come from the aristocratic, protected class.

Two additional techniques unique to Japanese poetry were first seen in the previous chapter: the makurakotoba, or pillow word, and kakekotoba, or pivot word. The epithetlike pillow words tended to be obscure—many were virtually incomprehensible even to classical-era readers—yet they cushioned their poems on qualities of sensual depth and the weight of ancient tradition. (One attempt to translate a pillow word is described on pages 73–75.)

The pivot word is a single word that carries two readings, each necessary to the full meaning of the poem. An example is *omoi*, "thinking" or "longing," which can be written in a way that indicates also the word for fire or burning. Another is "pine," *matsu* in Japanese, whose meanings—"pine tree" and "waiting"—are surprisingly close to the English homonyms. Overt punning of this kind almost never appears in a serious poem in English, but in classical Japanese poetry it was an important poetic device, used, like allusion and headnotes, to expand what may live in a thirty-one syllable house.

The pivot word's density and compression cannot be duplicated in translation, but its double meanings can be brought over, by explicit or implicit means. One poem by Ono no Komachi in which pivot words appear is discussed on pages 76–78; in another, English homonyms can render the pivot word *mirume*, which means both "seaweed" and "eyes of seeing":

A diver does not abandon
a seaweed-filled bay . . .
Surely you will not refuse

to see this floating, foam-white body,
that waits for your gathering hands.

Kakekotoba create a sense of the word, and the world, as multiple and fluid. In Komachi's poem, the imagination leaps between woman and kelp strands, between lover and diver. Within the logic of metaphor, the poem insists on her desirability, her irresistibility—and because in Komachi's time the ability to write such a poem was, in fact, an index of desirability, her words may well have had their intended effect.

With or without pivot words, Japanese poems virtually always proceed by such an imaginative transformation and alteration of being. In the shift of consciousness that occurs between outward phenomena and inner reflection, or between the circumstances of one thought and another, the heart-mind is remade. The leap may take place in metaphor, in narrative, in a pivot word. It may also be made through simple juxtaposition, two flashes of perception creating a virtually electric current between them:

Narcissus and screen:
one lights the other,
white on white.

In this haiku by Bashō, the technique is explicit: one thing is said to illuminate the other. Yet the true leap occurs in the seemingly still point of the final image. "White on white" has a mysterious depth, the phrase urging the reader to envision the elusive relationship between One and many; between relative, perishable flower and the absolute of the screen's rice-paper ground. "All things return to the One," a Zen koan states, then asks, "What does the One return to?" The answer is not to be found in the conceptual mind, yet it swims through this poem like a speckled trout through a stream.

W. S. Merwin has described haiku as "dynamic in the manner of a single frame of thought . . . the flash itself, immeasurable in any time whatever: no-time manifesting in time. So the movement of the haiku could be said not to move but to be, totally, movement. That movement which, because it is not relative, is inseparable from still-ness." Such movement inseparable from stillness lies at the center of Bashō's most famous haiku:

Old pond—
a frog jumps in:
splash-sound of water.

The old pond is completely an old pond, and also the awakened mind of Buddhist understanding. Timeless, imperturbable, and capa-cious, the water gives forth its sound without hesitation or question; in it, there is room for silence, there is room for sound. The poem goes back to Tsurayuki's question—upon hearing the singing of pond-dwelling frogs, who could fail to reply? To the world's unceasing query, this haiku is one answer. The frog leaps, Bashō writes. "Plop!" the onomatopoetic final phrase has been translated, as words disappear.

▾   ▾   ▾   ▾   ▾

B ETWEEN early tanka and Bashō's seventeenth-century haiku, a marked change occurred in poetic intention and tone. The transformation has its roots in the shifting development of Buddhist thought. During the beginning and middle periods of the Heian court, the most widely read Buddhist text was the Lotus Sutra. This sutra emphasizes the suffering born of impermanence and the release from suffering that various Buddhist teachings can bring. *Mujō*, tran-sience, is not named in Tsurayuki's preface as a central theme of the Heian poets. Perhaps it was so pervasive a concept that he did not even think to name it—as, for example, the Western sense of existence as teleological is similarly assumed in many literary texts. Yet mujō suffuses each example Tsurayuki offers when listing appropriate subjects for poems. Blossoms at dawn in spring, moonlit autumn nights, crimson leaves floating on a river—all are fleeting, changing phenomena. After several centuries, however, a new aesthetic appears, this time as a conscious goal: *yūgen,* a term for which there is no simple translation.

In *Japanese Court Poetry,* Robert Brower and Earl Miner describe yūgen's hallmarks as mystery and depth, and tell us that it is characterized by sadness, unspoken connotation, imagery of a veiled, monochromatic nature, and an atmosphere of haunting beauty. This representation seems itself a bit veiled; but even Fujiwara no Shunzei, the twelfth-century poet who first advocated its importance, never defined yūgen clearly, resorting instead to poetic circumambulation. A good poem, he wrote, will "possess a kind of atmosphere that is distinct from its words and their configuration and yet accompanies them. The atmosphere hovers over the poem, as it were, like the haze that trails over the cherry blossoms in spring, like the cry of the deer heard against the autumn moon, like the fragrance of spring in the flowering plum by the garden fence, like the autumn drizzle that drifts down upon the crimson foliage on some mountain peak" (trans. Robert Brower and Earl Miner).

It is hard from Shunzei's description to distinguish precisely what makes yūgen distinct, except that it seems to refer to some additional meaning that shimmers just outside a poem's expressed content. Yet there is another approach to the concept, alluded to by Brower and Miner and explored at length in a chapter of William R. LaFleur's *The Karma of Words.* According to this theory, the aesthetic of yūgen comes directly from the emergence in Japanese culture of Tendai Buddhism and its attending practice of *shikan* meditation. Related to the sense of "movement inseparable from stillness" that Merwin calls a hallmark of the later aesthetic of haiku, shikan might be described as a state in which the meditator rests—though one might equally well say "ranges"—in an undividing contemplation of what is. Its bare, transparent attention does not exclude the awareness of transience, but its core is the experience of nonduality, of the thorough interpenetration of self and Other.

Nonduality is not the negation of multiplicity in favor of some idea of the absolute; it is also not the nihilism so many Westerners think Buddhism to be. It is, in fact, no idea at all—remember that both Japanese poetry and the mind of meditation find their way not by means of abstraction but amid the bird cries and mountains of the phenomenal world. "Not one, not two" is a traditional phrase describing the nondual—but even these words of paradox cannot hold the experience of the dropping away of subjectively governed consciousness.

The nonseparation of Buddhist understanding lies close to the ground of all poetry, Western as well as Eastern. Every metaphor, every description that moves its reader, every hymn-shout of praise, points to the shared existence of beings and things. The mind of poetry makes visible how permeable we are to the winds and moonlight with which we share our house. There is a difference, though. In the consciousness of shikan meditation, there is nothing else: no words, no intermediate forms of attention or consciousness. Whatever is present becomes the entirety of what is. "Not one, not two."

The transparency of self that yūgen describes was not unknown to the earlier Heian-era poets. When Shikibu writes in one poem, "I cannot say which is which—the glowing plum blossom *is* the spring night's moon," the nondual mind is speaking. But the later aesthetic of yūgen asked that every poem carry within itself the mark of nondual perception. The result was a poetry more directly turned toward outward phenomena, while the overtly personal begins to recede, as in these tanka by Fujiwara no Teika (1162-1241), which both embody yūgen and look forward to the bareness and thusness that will come to characterize haiku:

> Look past the fragile blossoms,
> past crimson leaves—
> a thatched hut stands
> by an inlet,
> swallowed in autumn dusk.

And, even more haiku-like:

> A stalling ox,
> shuffling,
> swirls up dust—
> hot, even the wind,
> even the summer cart.
>
> *(trans. Hiroaki Sato)*

These two poems of sensory perception are not very different from a haiku written by Bashō roughly four centuries later, usually called his first mature poem:

> On a bare branch,
> a crow has landed:
> autumn nightfall.

If these later poems reflect back to their authors' lives—as every poem in some way does—it is in a fashion more complex and indirect than the earlier tanka. Their terrain tends more to states of being and consciousness than to the emotions arising in the course of daily life, and the keen sense of mourning, the grief at ephemerality present in so many early tanka, seems to have vanished. Over the centuries of Japanese literary endeavor, the poet's relationship to transience has altered: he has become one with the fleeting moment. It is a shift of

perception familiar to those who have undertaken intensive medita-
tion practice—sit long enough, quietly paying attention to what is
before you, and the mind-body's protests and self-regard will wear
themselves thin. Ego, pain, and the busy-work of conception settle,
ripples returning to pond. There, Bashō's frog-splash waits.

Yet human experience remains central to almost all of these poems.
When I first began to study the poetry of China and Japan, I thought
otherwise; my reading had led me to believe that Asian poetry's con-
tribution lay precisely in the way it turned to the outer world for mean-
ing rather than to the self. Nor is that conception entirely unfounded,
as a famous account of Bashō's teaching, written by his student Hattori
Toho, makes clear:

> "Learn about the pine from the pine, learn about the bamboo from the
> bamboo"—this dictum of our teacher means that you must forgo your
> subjectivity. If you interpret "learn" in your own way, you will end up
> not learning. To "learn" here means to enter the object; then if its
> essence reveals itself and moves you, you may come up with a verse.
> Even if you seem to have described the object, unless it has an emotion
> that comes out of it naturally, the object and your self will remain sep-
> arated, and the emotion you have described will not have attained sin-
> cerity, because it will be something made up by your subjectivity.
>
> (trans. Hiroaki Sato)

The description leans toward the outer object as both source and
end of a poem. But then we have Bashō's other advice to a disciple,
that the error in most poems is that they are either subjective or objec-
tive. Looking for clarification, the student asked, "Don't you mean too
objective or too subjective?" Bashō answered, simply, "No."

It is common sense. Take away a narrow subjectivity, and you will
also take away objectivity: there is no need to exclude the self when
the self is not selfish. What Bashō advocates comes not only from the

mind of Buddhist meditation, it is the way of union familiar to us from the reports of mystics from every tradition. The objectivity the poet must avoid is the reification of experience; a wrong subjectivity seeks to impose the narrow concerns of the self upon the world. Each approach misses the mark, because each is an act of oversimplification.

TRUTH and beauty live most happily amid complexity and paradox. Japanese poetry encompasses this knowledge in many ways: the long-familiar becomes the ground of the new; the precise seeds of the particular blossom into a field of suggestive fragrance; awareness of the fleeting leads to an understanding of interdependence and the continuity of being. A detached observation, the broad sweep of a passionate heart, and the workings of a deeply inquiring mind each contribute to how these poems are made. Such conjoined oppositions are the door and lintel of the house of Japanese poems: the wooden frame shaping the opening, and the opening shaping the frame.

But a turning knowledge is the hearth-fire, the aliveness at the center of the house. Such a turning appears—quietly, subtly, yet also with undeniable power—in this poem by Komachi:

How invisibly
it changes color
in this world,
the flower
of the human heart.

The poem can be read in two ways, as a general statement about human nature or as a poem about a relationship. The choice lies in one's interpretation of "in this world," *yo no naka*, which means literally "the world of the middle" or "the world of betweenness"; sometimes the phrase signifies the world of human beings and sometimes the world of love. In either case, the contrast is between the outer world's flowers, which lose their brilliance openly, and the shifting of human feeling, so easily concealed. Both actual flowers and the flower of the human heart must abide in continuous change—each is both lovely and transient. The poem knows bitterness, though, in the difference between them. Its unnamed grief burns like an icy current just below the surface of a sun-flecked river.

A poem by Izumi Shikibu, whose headnote tells us that it was written in the autumn during a time of retreat at a mountain temple, also turns on a widened seeing:

> Although I try
> to hold the single thought
> of Buddha's teaching in my heart,
> I cannot help but hear
> the many crickets' voices calling as well.

The poet is deep in her meditation when the night suddenly fills with the voices of crickets—small creatures exposed to the cold and dark, who will soon fall silent now that autumn has come. This poem, too, holds two possible interpretations; in this case, though, they are not alternative readings but readings made at different depths. At the surface level, the crickets are, as it seems, distraction: either the literal sounds of the world outside Shikibu's concentration, or, metaphorically, the persistent thoughts of her many lovers, continuing to call her toward erotic attachment. Even in this simple reading, the poem is moving—we feel for the poet, who, like the crickets, seems caught amid inescapable realms.

There is another way to read the poem, however, one that allows for a certain irony on the part of the poet. In this more complex reading, it is good that Shikibu hear these crickets and include their voice in her meditation. Buddhist awakening is not about excluding the world of human feeling but about perceiving how one moon shines in many dewdrops. "This very body, with all its passions, is itself the body of freedom," Zen teacher Dōgen said. In this understanding, a Buddhism that leaves out the voices of desire and transient, small creatures would be worthless. But the poem reports, that is all. It leaves the reader to discover the resonance between these two possible readings, to see that in the realm of the spiritual, as in the realm of poetry, only a cartoon can be simple. Whatever is real casts shadows.

Another poem of Shikibu's:

When the autumn wind
blows down from Tokiwa Mountain,
my body fills, as if blushing,
with the color and scent
of pine.

At first glance, the poem may seem an unshadowed conceit; again, though, multiple levels of understanding inhere. The mountain and wind and the green scent of pine are fully themselves and present. So too, perhaps, is the relationship that has caused the poet to be so acutely alert to her experience. Tokiwa Mountain's pine trees are an image long associated with love in Japanese poetry, and autumn can have many connotations. Always the true autumn of shortening days, it is a season that alludes as well to aging, sometimes of the self, sometimes of a relationship.

My first intuition is that the autumn of this poem points to a lover a good deal older than Shikibu. Shikibu juxtaposes the mountain pines' unchanging color with the shifting seasons of the rest of nature, of the human body and heart, and of time itself. The depth of the poem, then, lies in the contrast between what changes and ages and what does not. Not only do pine trees challenge the leaf-altering cold, the poet's body also is steadfast in her identification with their permanent greenness, and, in my allegorical reading of the poem, in her desire for a man who comes to her from the slopes of Tokiwa Mountain. It is a thought almost gallant in its resistance to the pressure of time. But the poem can also be read as just what it says: the poet's body, encountering the autumn wind, is dyed with the color and scent of pine. Her body and what the year's passage brings to it become one thing—a thought also near-gallant, but this time in its acceptance of the pressure of time.

In either interpretation, the mystery that fires this poem is the mystery that gives life to so many of these poems: the connection between human feeling and the nonhuman world of winds and trees and the green scent of needles. For the direction of Shikibu's perception moves as easily from outer life toward inner as the reverse. It is not just a matter of describing "inner" feeling through "outer" correlative. What we know of green-keeping love in the face of transience is also what binds us to the life of mountains, who speak with their own vocabulary and travel their own paths.

R. H. Blyth, in the preface to the fourth volume of his haiku translations, speaks of "something that belongs to the Japanese mind, the Japanese language, and the literature it produced and which produced it. We see it in linked poems, in the puns of the language of Nō, in the empty spaces of pictures, the absences of things in rooms, the silences of conversation. This 'something' is a certain continuity, a lack of division, a feeling of the whole when dealing with the parts."

The vast majority of Japanese poems were not written to address the relationship of self and other. Nor are they about transience, or any other idea. They are about what they seem to be about: individual, flickering moments of human feeling and consciousness and perception. About the pleasures, the playfulness, and the pain of love; about the prospect of aging, the death of a daughter, the first winter storm in November. But because they are utterly attentive, each to its moment, each to its part, the best of them do have the quality Blyth describes, a way of including the wholeness of life within a brief glimpse. These poems show us that a single moment's perception is more than enough to hold a world. It glitters, both beautiful and transient, amid the words' leaves.

Poetry and the Mind of Indirection

▾   ▾   ▾   ▾   ▾   ▾   ▾   ▾   ▾

A T T H E end of *Portrait of the Artist as a Young Man,* Stephen Dedalus renounces family, country, religion, everything that has been familiar to him, and vows to take up his new path as artist with "the only arms I allow myself to use: silence, exile, and cunning."

This motto—which Richard Ellman tells us Joyce took from Balzac, and Balzac (ironically enough, given Stephen's renunciation of Catholicism) from the Carthusian order of monks—is useful for any aspiring writer of prose. It is more apt still for a poet. Not for poetry the head-on meeting of inquiry and object found in the essay, the debate, or the letter to the editor. A poem circles its content, calls to it from afar, looks for the hidden, tangential approach, the truth that grows apparent only by means of exile's wanderings, cunning's imagination, and a wide-cast, attentive silence. Poems do not make appointments with their subjects—they stalk them, keeping their distance, looking slightly off to one side. And when at last the leap comes, it is most often also from the side, the rear, an overhead perch; from some word-blind woven of brush or shadow or fire.

Why do circuitousness and indirection play so great a role in poetic thought? One hint lies in the very metaphor of hunting: only when looked at from a place of asideness and exile does the life of the world step fully forward. There is a shyness at the core of existence, a hesitance to be seen. Even domestic animals do not like having their pictures taken. By removing the self from the landscape through silence and stillness—the same silence and stillness that lead to concentration—the watcher begins to perceive "from the point of view of the animal," as José Ortega y Gasset wrote in his *Meditations on Hunting*. It is an essential alteration. When we begin to see the landscape as the animals themselves see it, undistorted by clamorous self-assertion, a widened constellation of being emerges to graze and root and swim.

Traveling this way of obliqueness, at times even the poet does not recognize his prey, mistaking camouflage and quarry: the self's deepest ponderings must often be taken by ambush. When, at a celebration in Robert Frost's honor, one admiring critic alluded to death as Frost's true subject, the poet vehemently denied it; T. S. Eliot famously insisted that his work came in no way from his life. But consciousness and intention do not have the final say in poems: journey far enough in the terrain of language, it seems, and the heart will begin to speak.

In poetry's hunting, both the fugitive prey and the arrow are double in nature. Each has a life in the world beyond the page; each also lives wholly by words. Language is sought, and seeks. The poet, pursuing a vessel to hold something known, finds what the poem may know that the poet as yet does not. Poetry's grammars, strategies, and language have their own wisdom—entering its woods, we find ourselves living with thought-forms that feed only within the ways of the leafy and hidden.

Consider Apollo and Daphne. Apollo, tamer of the wild Muses

and patron-god of poetry, pursued Daphne without pause. When the nymph realized she could not escape, she begged the earth-goddess Gaia for rescue. At his moment of triumph, then, Apollo found in his arms not the beautiful warm-fleshed nymph but a woman rough-skinned and cooling: becoming a tree, a laurel, whose leaves would become in turn his wreath of honor. There are things we can possess only by following them into the realm of disguise. There, we may be given a quarry altered, more pungent and wilder and stranger than we had surmised.

SILENCE, exile, and cunning—you may ask, is something not missing from this list? Surely the realizations we have come to call "art" depend on the presence of the creative as well. Yet at the deepest level, not just art but all forms of thought, even simple perception itself, require the creative mind. In *Art and Visual Perception*, Rudolph Arnheim describes the most simple seeing as "imaginative, inventive, shrewd, and beautiful." Because recognition depends on a grasping of place and function within an overall pattern, Arnheim says, "all perceiving is also thinking; all reasoning is also intuition; all observation is also invention." Elsewhere, he puts it more concisely still: "Eyesight is insight." Perhaps the invention innate to every act of perception explains the joyous visual ornamentation found from the beginning in every human community. So deeply is creativity a part of human knowing that not only sacred offerings but donkey baskets, cooking pots, even the body's surface, require spirals, colors, patterns, before they are considered ready for use.

Language-making is a creative patterning as well. Of the relationship between inchoate, flowing phenomena and the corresponding map of language, Benjamin Whorf wrote in *Language, Thought, and Reality:*

The world is presented in a kaleidoscopic flux of impressions which has to be organized by our minds—and this means largely by the linguistic systems in our minds. We cut nature up, organize it into concepts, and ascribe significances as we do, largely because we are parties to an agreement to organize it this way—an agreement that holds throughout our speech community and is codified in the patterns of our language.

Traditional Buddhist thought prefigures the linguists, proposing that what we think "real" is instead the construct of an assembling consciousness. While a person may act as if the apparent exists, one with awakened understanding remains aware of the provisionality of that existence, taking the points of view of the made and the Unmade at the same time. The flavor of this way of thinking is not easy to capture, but over the centuries a lexicon of hints has accumulated, in word-images such as "gateless gate" and "snow in a silver bowl," or statements like Dōgen's "Ashes are ashes, firewood is firewood; firewood does not become ash, nor ashes return to wood." These phrases encircle their knowledge in words that can be pondered, turned over in the mind until they grow suddenly translucent and ripe. Within their indirection, paradox, and metaphors, speech brushes against its far limits.

We have already seen that virtually all language emerges from just such metaphorical thinking. Look at the statement itself: "Virtually all language emerges from just such metaphorical thinking" seems entirely abstract, yet within its words hidden riches of metaphor spiral. The most fundamental metaphor, and so the closest to invisible, lies in the verb *emerges*—a spatial description for a process that does not, in fact, occur in the dimensional world. But there are others as well: buried in the etymologies of individual words we find the shining, erratically surfacing ore of the physical body. In *language,* the fleshy tongue speaks; in *virtually,* there lingers a faint remnant of its root in the idea of strength. *Emerge* rises from *merge*, which originally meant to dive, or to dip something, into water. Kin to immerse and submerge, to emerge is to step from the lake of the One and become a "one," individual and alone. And finally there is *metaphor* itself—"to carry beyond." Metaphor is the way language carries itself past its own powers, to enter new realms.

But if creative making lives in our every mental gesture, both verbal and nonverbal, what then *is* particular to the kinds of perception we call art? First, art springs from a heightening, widening, and deepening of attention, and a craft-sense sufficiently developed to place this altered condition into the work. Second, the artist's deepened concentration lets what may have previously been difficult to see enter the realm of the knowable and so be made available, to both artist and others. And third, a work of art hews more closely than everyday thought to the cunning, circuitous nature of our most basic mental strategies. It arises from deep structures of comprehension that are continually at work within us but are only noticed when the processes of understanding become as significant as its ends. Art's seeming obliquenesses and riddling meanderings are not arbitrary—the circuitousness of artistic form is what appears once conventionalized habits of mind are stripped off, allowing the deeper grain to be revealed.

TO RECOGNIZE imaginative encirclement as a primary mode of thought is to remake one's relationship to knowing. It is to understand that the cognitive tropes particular to poetry are as aboriginal as its music—not illustration, not the ornamentation of abstract thought, but central devices for ordering the plenitude of being. Western culture, utilitarian by long practice and desire, believes in "cold facts," and such thinking brings its gifts. But the mind's primary knowing is hot, as fluid and protean as the changing magma of the earth. Art, by its very existence, undoes the idea that there can be only one description of the real, some single and simple truth on whose surface we may thoughtlessly walk. The intelligence that simmers in stories, paintings, and poems warns us: if the mind of art cannot entirely be trusted, nor can the ground.

From the Greek myths, from Shakespeare, from African folklore, we can see it: the unreliability of the apparent is one of narrative's core themes. Tales of mistaken twins, of sweetly phrased lies, of riddles read wrongly, abound. The deceit within stories, the deceit of story itself, is another disclosure of artful circuitousness, one that instructs us in the vulnerability of our own thought. Narrative's fictions and fidelities can be as dangerous as the practice of politics by anecdote, or as accurate a penetration of society's realms as exists in the prose of Kafka. Like the Sirens, narrative sings us into a journey that is disaster and beauty both, steering us onto the harsh rocks of the world's mixed wisdom.

Story is the spinning wheel on which continuity is spliced, source of our sense of self. Narrative's yarn is also the substance with which a culture addresses its questions: religion and science each sleep in a cradle woven and hung upon stories. By its place in the pattern, we learn which information is more significant, which less; though anything mentioned has meaning—as it must, in a universe in which each thing is tied to everything else. Any individual construct may be suspect, but without story, we cannot live as humans do.

Often, the stories we hold about self and world are subliminal, wielding the power of the unexamined, and thus go unquestioned. But the shaping of art is also a way such hidden narratives are softened, made workable; it brings them into a kind of attention that reaches both conscious and unconscious minds. And so, as a culture's needs shift, its stories alter. Old myths shape-shift, new ones come forth. Figures in fairy tales begin to live in cottages, not just in the palaces of heroic myth; women protagonists step into their own point of view and powers. Further, narrative hunts out the seed-events that hold a useful knowledge for our lives. In its portable woven pouch, it places the moments that count and also carries the fact that there are moments that count.

One example of such a knowledge-holding work is Robert Hass's prose poem, "A Story About the Body":

> The young composer, working that summer at an artist's colony, had watched her for a week. She was Japanese, a painter, almost sixty, and he thought he was in love with her. He loved her work, and her work was like the way she moved her body, used her hands, looked at him directly when she made amused and considered answers to his questions. One night, walking back from a concert, they came to her door and she turned to him and said, "I think you would like to have me. I would like that too, but I must tell you that I have had a double mastectomy," and when he didn't understand, "I've lost both my breasts." The radiance that he had carried around in his belly and chest cavity—like music—withered very quickly, and he made himself look at her when he said, "I'm sorry. I don't think I could." He walked back to his own cabin through the pines, and in the morning he found a small blue bowl on the porch outside his door. It looked to be full of rose petals, but he found when he picked it up that the rose petals were on top; the rest of the bowl—she must have swept them from the corners of her studio—was full of dead bees.

There is no way to paraphrase what is stored in this account, and I can think of no other piece, poetry or prose, that touches on what it tells. Like any good story, it is not just one tale, but many. It is the tale of its images, of its events, of its clarities and misunderstandings. It is the tale of the two artists, and of the desire, pride, dignity, tact, and shame swimming through them. It is the tale of the speaker who gives us the story withholding all comment, and of the reader's own inescapable wondering, "What would I have done, if I were her, if I were him? How do I weigh these two?" Japanese poetry speaks of a poem's *nioi*, its fragrance, and its *hibiki*, reverberation, as qualities equal in standing to its "content." To recognize the way such powers and essences work in this poem is to taste the irreducibility as well as the circularity of art.

A SMALL blue bowl of petals and bees: unsurpassable gift. Receiving such an image, or even a poem's music, we do so within the permeable and roving mind of indirection and metaphor, that finds in one thing the informing radiance of another. Rose petals, dead bees, have meaning. Surface and undersurface have meaning. They do not need spelling out for us to understand.

Within a good poem is the elegance scientists speak of when they describe a solution both economical and true. Cleaving close to the ground rules by which all language is made, good poetry carries broad information within brief speech. Image in particular, by gathering many energies toward a single end, creates an intense compression of meaning; it carries into the mind the solidity, particularity, and multifacetedness of actual objects. Such concreteness is a handle: it can be grasped. It must also be turned. That turning opens the reader into a place of enlarged awareness, where different connotations may resonate together. Before the slipperiness of unformed thought, the image offers purchase; to the stolidity of things, it offers imagination's alchemical, stirring powers.

This elegance of means makes even the sparest poetry beautiful. Like an honest grocer, such a poem gives good weight. The mind's innate capacity for indirection allows one thing to speak for others; through that open gate, the unspoken gains entrance into the poem. Poetry, Pound has written, is compression. By how much is left out, we may measure how much is there. This aspect of poetry, too, involves wandering and indirection: to read a poem well, we must travel through its words but also pass through its silences, into the unlocked storehouse of self. Not everything will be given—some part of a poem's good weight will be found outside the poem, in us. All image in this way involves the mind of metaphor: it is only tasted and understood when carried into the self.

"I Would Like to Describe," by the Polish poet Zbigniew Herbert, looks closely at image and statement, at direct and indirect speech:

I would like to describe the simplest emotion
joy or sadness
but not as others do
reaching for shafts of rain or sun

I would like to describe a light
which is being born in me
but I know it does not resemble
any star
for it is not so bright
not so pure
and it is uncertain

I would like to describe courage
without dragging behind me a dusty lion
and also anxiety
without shaking a glass full of water

to put it another way
I would give all metaphors
in return for one word
drawn out of my breast like a rib
for one word
contained within the boundaries
of my skin

but apparently this is not possible

and just to say—I love
I run around like mad
picking up handfuls of birds
and my tenderness
which after all is not made of water
asks the water for a face

and anger
different from fire
borrows from it
a loquacious tongue

so is blurred
so is blurred
in me
what white-haired gentlemen
separated once and for all
and said
this is the subject
and this is the object

we fall asleep
with one hand under our head
and with the other in a mound of planets

our feet abandon us
and taste the earth
with their tiny roots
which next morning
we tear out painfully

(trans. Czeslaw Milosz and Peter Dale Scott)

What is hidden in daily speech is here played out—language's utter dependence on comparative mind. Herbert's longing for "one simple word" is a true impulse; it is also an unattainable dream. A metaphor not dusty with age or simplified to the point of lying is all one can finally ask. For in truth, this "one word / drawn out of my breast like a rib," "contained within the boundaries / of my skin," is unattainable precisely because its existence would refute what we already know: underlying the mind of language is the undeniable interconnection of each thing and being of earth. The loneliness of Herbert's imagined single word would be unbearable.

To be sure, the "white-haired gentlemen" of the rational mind, busily dissecting subject and object, are a good part of our humanness, and Herbert does not deny them. But he also will not refuse that other knowledge: that we live in the body, and in the body's instinctive reaching-out into the rest of existence. Depending on one's point of view, such interconnection may prove us more than human, or less. Yet in those "tiny roots" is a tenderness only approachable when lion, bird, water, and fire are each allowed in.

The circuitousness of this poem is at least two-fold. Its subject and imagery rest in the mind of metaphoric language, requiring us to circle from poem and self into the world of the other. But obliqueness appears as well at the level of rhetoric: by using a verbal strategy of seemingly reluctant self-correction to make his point, the poet makes that point also poignant, hard-won. Emotion, like language, is never "simple"; nor is the poet's attempt to convey meaning; nor is the truth of who and what we are. And that last, of course, is the poem's real subject, approached through an apparent exploration of the nature of speech and metaphor—that is, indirectly. Again we see it: circumambulating their subject is the way poems know.

▾   ▾   ▾   ▾   ▾

Many writers have addressed the circuitous nature of thought. Among them is the eighteenth-century German poet and aphorist Novalis, who wrote, "Perceptibility is a kind of attentiveness."

Novalis's statement first caught my attention in John Berger's *Ways of Seeing*. What startled was the choice of "perceptibility" rather than "perception." To say that perception is attentiveness is almost a tautology. But to say that perceptibility—the ability to *be* known—is the result of attention paid out, that is interesting. We see, this reading of the aphorism proposes, because what we see sees us: "For here, there is no place that does not look back," reads one translation of Rilke's "Archaic Torso of Apollo." In this radical vision of vision, there is no difference between human and nonhuman, between sentient and nonsentient. All being becomes single, alive, available, and awake.

A different choice of stress, and so of meaning, can also be found in Novalis's sentence. Perceptibility is a *kind* of attentiveness: the way that you look at a thing and who you are determine what you will see. That thought appears also in William Blake's reply to a patron who complained of a lack of "realistic" content in his work:

> I see Every thing I paint in This world, but Every body does not see alike. To the Eyes of a Miser a Guinea is far more beautiful than the Sun, & a bag worn with the use of Money has more beautiful proportions than a Vine filled with Grapes. The tree which moves some to tears of joy is in the Eyes of others only a Green thing which stands in the way. Some see Nature all Ridicule & Deformity, and by these I shall not regulate my proportions; & some scarce see Nature at all. But to the Eyes of the Man of Imagination, Nature is Imagination itself. As a man is, so he sees. As the Eye is formed, such are its Powers.

"There is a whole portion of reality"—here it is Ortega y Gasset, in *Meditations of Quixote*—

> which is offered to us without our making any special effort beyond opening our eyes and ears, and this we call the world of pure impressions. But there is another world built of structures of impressions, which, though hidden, is none the less real. If this other world is to

exist for us, we need to open something more than our physical eyes, and to undertake a greater kind of effort. But the measure of our effort neither confers any reality on that world, nor takes it away. The deep world is as clear as the surface one, only it asks more of us.

(adapted from a trans. by J. W. Jeaffreson)

"Words are probes," Ludwig Wittgenstein wrote in one of his notebooks on January 23, 1915. "Some reach very deep, some only to a little depth." Novalis, Blake, and Ortega each propose that the difference in depth lies not in the words, but in the way that we answer the deep world's request for "more." It is the request of the biblical injunction, "Heed that which you hear: the measure you give is the measure you will receive," and of the Talmudic saying, "We do not see things as they are, we see them as we are." Then there is Dickinson: "Not 'Revelation'—'tis—that waits, / But our unfurnished eyes—" and Picasso's startling prescription: "It is in fact only love that matters, in whatever it may be. They should put out the eyes of painters as they do those of bullfinches, to make them sing better."

Both readings of Novalis's aphorism—that an awareness resides in the things we wish to observe and know, and that the way we come to them matters—enter into a letter by Rilke, sent in the winter of 1920 to Baladine Klossowska, a lover and fellow writer with whom he shared a passionate correspondence:

These Things whose essential life you want to express first ask you, "Are you free? Are you prepared to devote all your love to me . . . ?" And if the Thing sees that you are otherwise occupied with even a particle of your interest, it shuts itself off; it may perhaps give you some slight sign of friendship, a word or a nod, but it will never give you its heart, entrust you with its patient being, its sweet sidereal constancy, which makes it so like the constellations in the sky. In order for a Thing to speak to you, you must regard it for a certain time as *the only one that exists*, as the one and only phenomenon which, through your laborious and exclusive love, is now placed at the center of the universe, and which, in that incomparable place, is on that day attended by angels.

(trans. Stephen Mitchell)

This passage about art is also artful: seductively infused with the circumstances of its writing. Words describing the writer's necessary commitment to his subject blush through with their other intention, to further the discourse of love. Nor are the two concerns unrelated— more than a superficial resemblance connects the making of art to the making of love, not least the felt presence of an Other.

Finally, Rilke's suggestions recall Bashō's precept, "Learn about the pine from the pine, learn about the bamboo from the bamboo." Each poet, in his own language, states that the basic matter of poetry comes not from the self, but from the world. From Things, which will speak to us on their own terms and with their own wisdom, but only when approached with our full and unselfish attention.

▾   ▾   ▾   ▾   ▾

ATTENTIVENESS, and even craft, are not the same as will. Knowing and not-knowing are equal parents to a poem: to learn from what lies outside the self requires stepping beyond what lies within. Frost described the poet's work as wandering through a field, allowing those burrs that will to stick to his pants—an apt illustration of the meanderings of mind that are integral to the process of writing. "Result of chance; fruit of calculation," is Octavio Paz's description of a poem, a subtle balancing act—*result*, the colder term, with its links to the idea of cause and effect, is coupled with *chance;* while *fruit*, carrying the natural world's fragrance and richness, its unselfconscious sense of gift, accompanies *calculation*.

Craft and consciousness matter. But a poet's attention must also be open to what is not already understood, decided, weighed out. For a poem to be fully alive, the poet needs to surrender the protection of the known and venture into a different relationship with the subject—or is it object? both words miss—of her attention. The poet must learn from what dwells outside her conceptions, capacities, and even language: from exile and silence.

The rich sustenance the unknown offers can be traced explicitly in poems of different cultures and times. From *Gilgamesh* and the *Odyssey* through the Grail poems and on, the epic hero must travel into strange lands and unforeseeable events in order to become what he is. Even that other hero, Penelope, is ripened by her ignorance of Odysseus's fate as much as by her hope for his return. Her fidelity is a fabric of unweaving and unknowing, not mere refusal; who more than she has dwelled in uncertainty, free of the irritable reaching after fact?

But more often, the archetype appears in descriptions of literal vulnerability and wandering, Odysseus's physical journey. To understand the world beyond the narrow self, such poems say, it is necessary to expose that self to the unmapped and the uncontrolled, to be touched by it and transformed. It is by jeopardy, not invulnerability, that the hero matures. Habit, laziness, and fear conspire to keep us comfortably within the familiar. There we may make our way in the dark and never stumble against an unexpected wall, into an unexpected stairwell or door. But if we would seek a widened knowledge, the accumulated lore of poetry tells us, it is necessary first to stand in the open.

Not only the heroic epic touches this theme. One brief poem by Izumi Shikibu about vulnerability has already been quoted:

It is true the wind
blows terribly here—
but moonlight also leaks
between the roof planks
of this ruined house.

Then there is the beginning of Dante's *Divine Comedy*, which also informs that wisdom comes only after we surrender the state of protection:

> Midway on our life's journey, I found myself
>   In dark woods, the right road lost. To tell
>   About those woods is hard—so tangled and rough
>
> And savage that thinking of it now, I feel
>   The old fear stirring: death is hardly more bitter.
>   And yet, to treat the good I found there as well
>
> I'll tell what I saw . . .
>
> *(trans. Robert Pinsky)*

With this passage about leaving the manmade road for a place both chaotic and frightening, the poet abandons all order and safety. He steps into the solitude and darkness of a wilderness beyond measure. Yet everything Dante goes on to see and learn has its roots in this departure: only the passage through such a place—through the circles of hell itself—leads to the knowledge of paradise.

In tragedy, as well, lost places are sites for the soul's instruction. The first words of *Macbeth* give the scene as "An open place. Thunder and Lightning," and the first characters onstage are those outsider-beings, the Witches. In *King Lear*, inner and outer madness join amid a raging storm as Lear and his companions wander the heath, and *Hamlet*'s opening scene lies on—not within—the walls of the castle; its speechless ghost breathes into the play the dispossessed, sorrowful knowledge of the beyond. There is also the opening of Racine's *Phèdre*, in which Hippolytus, not knowing how true his vow will prove, proclaims:

> No, no, my friend, we're off! Six months have passed
> since Father heard the ocean howl and cast

his galley on the Aegean's skull-white froth.
Listen! The blank sea calls us—off, off, off!
I'll follow Father to the fountainhead
and marsh of hell. We're off. Alive or dead,
I'll find him.

(trans. Robert Lowell)

And finally, to bring the theme to the current century, there is Robinson Jeffers's "Carmel Point," which praises the unhumanized world as a storehouse of wisdom:

The extraordinary patience of things!
This beautiful place defaced with a crop of suburban houses—
How beautiful when we first beheld it,
Unbroken field of poppy and lupin walled with clean cliffs;
No intrusion but two or three horses pasturing,
Or a few milch cows rubbing their flanks on the outcrop rockheads—
Now the spoiler has come: does it care?
Not faintly. It has all time. It knows the people are a tide
That swells and in time will ebb, and all
Their works dissolve. Meanwhile the image of the pristine beauty
Lives in the very grain of the granite,
Safe as the endless ocean that climbs our cliff. —As for us:
We must uncenter our minds from ourselves;
We must unhumanize our views a little, and become confident
As the rock and ocean that we were made from.

Each of these works is different in language, in technique, in aesthetic and philosophical tradition, yet in each the same insight appears. To see the world truly, we need a consciousness that has been steeped in more than the human—that has traveled away from the tamed, from the familiar, from the narrow limits of self. Starting on such a path, difficulty and hardship are all that is promised, yet the knowledge gained on such a journey need not always be tragic.

Sometimes it is joyous, as Emily Dickinson (who also knew the fearsome falling of reason unplanked) reported:

Exultation is the going
Of the inland soul to sea—
Past the houses, past the headlands,
Into deep Eternity.

▼   ▼   ▼   ▼   ▼

O<small>F</small> Stephen Dedalus's three-part strategy there remains still silence, the poem's other, brimming state.

BUT A poem is never entirely silent, and in poetry, silence may also speak. Poetry's fertility lives in the marriage of said and unsaid, of languaged self and unlanguaged other, of the knowable world and the gravitational pull of what lies beyond knowing. At times, as in Hopkins, the unspoken presses up in a denseness weighted to the point of fracture. In Paul Celan, an unwordable knowledge gnaws the thread of language almost—yet never entirely—through. Dickinson's many different types of dashes are a visible breaking in of the underlying silence all thought is wrung from—the light silences of mind regathering for the next forward surge, the unnavigable silence that ends a poem midstride. There is the surrounding silence in which the work of poetry takes place, the richly active silence of listening and of the reader's necessary addition. Then there is the silence of which George Steiner wrote: "Where the word of the poet ceases, a great light begins."

▼·　▼　▼　▼　▼

In Chuang-tzu's *The Way and Its Power,* Arthur Waley has pointed out, the phrase "returning to the Nameless" is written with ideograms that can also be read as "to get into the birdcage without setting the birds off singing." This "secret language" of Taoist teaching is poetry's language—to speak of silence, poetry tiptoes past birds. Not because there is no other way, but because in the fragile silence of sleeping birds, the nameless is deepened. And, too, because the nature of returning to what lies beyond words is made visible by the metaphorical task—it summons from within the body's own knowledge what care and concentration will be required.

To enter the cage without setting the birds off singing is the strategy, too, of poetry as a whole. Those interior birds, like the geese some farmers keep as avian watchdogs, are Zbigniew Herbert's white-haired guardians of rational, logical mind, defending against the more permeable life that poetry calls into being. Poetry steals its way into meaning; by the time the intruder is recognized, the task is already accomplished. A poem is a detour we willingly subject ourselves to, a trick surprising us into the deepened vulnerability we both desire and fear. Its strategies of beauty, delay, and deception smuggle us past the border of our own hesitation. There is reason to fear: a great poem, like a great love, challenges our solitude, our conceptions, the very ground of being. Encountering such a poem, we tremble a little as we enter its gates. But the end, as in love, is to know and feel what could not be known or felt by any path less demanding.

In Japanese, the words sometimes respectively translated as *mind* and *heart* are suffused with the other's nature in a way that English speakers can scarcely conceive. The heart thinks; the mind feels keenly. In poetry, mind, emotion, body, and perception are similarly entwined, each circling into the realm of the others, part of a whole. Such interweaving forges an imaginative understanding in which language is not so much the object of attention as an act of attention played out, before us and in us: poetry's hearing and seeing as well as speaking.

What a good poem hears, sees, and speaks is what can only become perceptible when inner and outer intertwine. The poet's circuitous collaboration with words is a tool for discovering how best to let those two worlds come forward and realize themselves; it is part of the ancient, ongoing game of hide and seek the universe plays. Within its silence, exile, and cunning, poetry holds both the hiding and the seeking, for both are the point. Within its thicket of indirections is shelter for the elusive, independent animals of interconnected life. They pass overhead and underfoot, in and out of the trees and the dappled light that blossoms as well in barred feathers and spotted pelts. They are such shy or bold creatures as come into poetry's word-set nets, to be seen, to be finally eaten: to disappear into and become us, and so allow us also to become them—animal, vegetable, mineral, word, all thoroughly mysterious and known.

Two Secrets: On Poetry's Inward and Outward Looking

▼　▼　▼　▼　▼　▼　▼　▼　▼　▼

A FEW fully realized poems exist in which no glimpse of the outer world's landscape appears. Think of Catullus's famous "Odi et Amo":

> I hate and I love.
> Ask, if you wish,
> why this is so—
> I can't say.
> But I feel it
> and I am in torment.

Or Bertolt Brecht's "I, The Survivor":

> I know of course: it's simply luck
> That I've survived so many friends. But last night in a dream
> I heard those friends say of me: "Survival of the fittest"
> And I hated myself.

> *(trans. John Willet)*

Or "Che Fece . . . Il Gran Refiuto," by Cavafy:

> For some people the day comes
> when they have to declare the great Yes
> or the Great No. It's clear at once who has the Yes
> ready within him; and saying it,
>
> he goes forward in honor and self-assurance.
> He who refuses does not repent. Asked again,
> he would still say no. Yet that no—the right no—
> undermines him all his life.
>
> *(trans. Edmund Keeley and Philip Sherrard)*

And Celan's:

> You were my death:
> you could be held,
> when from me everything fell.

It is hard to pin down how these poems of pure statement so move the reader, but a good part of their power lies in embraced tension, the way they pull in more than a single direction. Each poem makes a knot, both in what is said and also in the insight it offers into something that cannot in the end be wholly named, only approached. And bare though they are of outward sensory image, these direct-speaking poems do have a sense realm—the kinesthetic. They are muscled with the almost cellular consciousness by which an oak grows into its own leaning, taking into account the stone that holds the roots, the various weights of foliage, acorn, snow.

Such purely internal poems are rare, and usually brief; most need some recourse to the outer world in order to speak. An explanation lies in the word *idea,* from *idein,* the Greek verb meaning "to see." In its connection of vision and thought we find the first secret of poetry's ability to quarry knowledge by mining the outer for inner ore. The linkage appears in other forms as well—"I see" is in English a synonym for "I understand."

Through actively perceptive speech, outer world and inner experience collaborate in the creation of meaning. For Dickinson, sorrow comes in slanted winter light that falls "like the weight / Of cathedral tunes." Blake finds the world's fierceness in the blazing body of a tiger and describes joy as a thing to be kissed as it flies. Wallace Stevens, even when speaking of something fundamentally abstract, embodies his statement, and so writes, paradoxically, "There is no wing like meaning." To speak as these poets do, with a precise tongue and unbounded eye, is to liberate things as well as ourselves into a greater aliveness.

The catalyzing energies of the outer do not require metaphor or simile. There is vital and mysterious power in even the simple, concrete details of an anonymous Egyptian woman's love poem, written around 1500 BCE:

> I find my love fishing
> His feet in the shallows.
>
> We have breakfast together
> And drink beer.
>
> I offer him the magic of my thighs
> He is caught in the spell.
> *(trans. Ezra Pound and Noel Stock)*

The cool water washing over the man's feet, the breakfast beer— these sensuous details entrance the reader into the poem, as the lover himself is entranced into the relationship. In much the same way, Sappho uses the promise of sensual beauty to lure Aphrodite to Lesbos in the seventh century BCE:

Leave Crete,
Aphrodite,
and come to this
sacred place
encircled by apple trees,
fragrant with offered smoke.

Here, cold springs
sing softly
amid the branches;
the ground is shady with roses;
from trembling young leaves,
a deep drowsiness pours.

In the meadow,
horses are cropping
the wildflowers of spring,
scented fennel
blows on the breeze.

In this place,
Lady of Cyprus, pour
the nectar that honors you
into our cups,
gold, and raised up for drinking.

In each of these poems, nature simply is. The horses grazing on wildflowers are horses grazing on wildflowers, the murmur of water is murmuring water—their meaning is their own existence, nothing more. Yet within them lies also the irresistible seduction of Being itself. That is why desirable landscapes suffuse the poetry of courtship, whether what is courted is human lover or sacred Other: intimacy occurs not only within the body of ankle, breast, and thigh, but also within the large body of earth.

▾   ▾   ▾   ▾   ▾

Outer images carry reflective and indirect meanings as well. Poems of this kind—the great majority of poems, that is—generally take one of three possible stances. In the first stance, outer reference serves the poet's interior thinking: the world beyond the self appears, but the relationship is that of monologue, with a human-centered consciousness dominating. In the second stance, the poet and the outer world stand face to face in mutual regard; out of that meeting, the poem's statements arise. Here the relationship is that of dialogue, with the wider world treated as both equal and other. In the third stance, the poet becomes an intermediary, a medium through whom the world of objects and nature beyond human consciousness may speak; in poetry's transparent and active transcription, language itself becomes an organ of perception.

We can think of these three stances as the subjective, reflective, and objective modes. Naming them this way, one might envision a hierarchy—might think that the subjective voice is necessarily self-centered and immature, the voice of reflection a little wiser, and the objective voice the fruit of a thoroughly ripened consciousness. It may well be so. But such judging is not entirely useful; better to contemplate all three, and see what true work each can do.

The subjective mode does carry a particular risk. The lapse into solipsism, pitfall of the worst Romantic poems, continues to throw a sentimental fog over many people's idea of what poetry is. An example of the subjective stance's potential for failure is Shelley's "The Cloud":

> I bring fresh showers for the thirsting flowers,
>   From the seas and the streams;

I bear light shade for the leaves when laid
    In their noonday dreams.
From my wings are shaken the dews that waken
    The sweet buds every one,
When rocked to rest on their mother's breast,
    As she dances about the sun . . .

The poem does not improve. Its anthropomorphizing conscious-
ness has become untenable to contemporary ears, and even its rhythms
lack depth. Yet in other poems of the first stance, subjective meaning
can inhabit the realm of the other with both humility and accuracy. In
"Window," by Czeslaw Milosz, a tree (whose actual existence the
reader readily trusts) primarily stands for the poet's self:

I looked out the window at dawn and saw a young apple tree
    translucent in brightness.

And when I looked out at dawn once again, an apple tree laden
    with fruit stood there.

Many years had probably gone by but I remember nothing of
    what happened in my sleep.

            (trans. Czeslaw Milosz and Lillian Vallee)

One difference between "Window" and "The Cloud" is that Milosz
does not turn to personification: the tree may be primarily interior in
its meaning, but the poet's own presence in the poem assures us that
he does not pretend to be it, or pretend that the realm of the natural
can be simply subsumed into the human. Yet even this latter strategy
can sometimes succeed without stripping the dignity from things—
another work in the subjective mode is Louise Glück's *The Wild Iris.*
A book of radical ventriloquism in which personification is ubiqui-
tous, its poems speak in three voices: the voice of a somewhat distant
creator; of a human speaker; and of the inhabitants of the poet's

garden—the hawthorn tree, the various lilies, snowdrops, violets, iris, trillium. Every part of the chorus is clearly part of the speaker's psyche, but Glück's unabashed personification never entails the distortion of nature into self that so disturbs in Shelley. Instead, we feel the book as an attempt to project the self as far as possible into the Other, with the goal of exploring that self from the broadest possible perspective, as in "Witchgrass":

Something
comes into the world unwelcome
calling disorder, disorder—

If you hate me so much
don't bother to give me
a name: do you need
one more slur
in your language, another
way to blame
one tribe for everything—

as we both know,
if you worship
one god, you only need
one enemy—

I'm not the enemy.
Only a ruse to ignore
what you see happening
right here in this bed,
a little paradigm
of failure. One of your precious flowers
dies here almost every day
and you can't rest until
you attack the cause,

meaning
whatever is left, whatever
happens to be sturdier
than your personal passion—

It was not meant
to last forever in the real world.
But why admit that, when you can go on
doing what you always do,
mourning and laying blame,
always the two together.

I don't need your praise
to survive. I was here first,
before you were here, before
you ever planted a garden.
And I'll be here when only the sun and moon
are left, and the sea, and the wide field.

I will constitute the field.

The voice is unquestionably human in its qualities and its pur-
poses, yet a tremendous energy comes into this poem from its passage
through the imagined consciousness of the grass. The last line, in par-
ticular, has the authority of the wild, and the chilling nonnegotiability
of the wild. (Such nonnegotiability is one definition of wildness:
though genetic near-kin, a caribou treated like the long-domesticated
reindeer will quickly die of stress.) Further, there is nothing frivolous
in Glück's technique: in her poems, personification is an essential tool
for discovery. Poets throughout history have turned to animal and
mineral being to express their own because from that storehouse a
larger vocabulary of being, particularity, and wisdom can emerge.

Wholly symbolic or allegorical poems also fall within the subjec-
tive mode. In Blake's song of experience, "The Sick Rose," nature
seems hardly nature at all:

O rose, thou art sick!
The invisible worm
That flies in the night,
In the howling storm,

Has found out thy bed
Of crimson joy,
And his dark secret love
Does thy life destroy.

This poem's rose grows from no earthly soil and its worm is no ordinary garden pest, yet still we can recognize why Blake enlists these things in his diagnosis of the human soul. What besides image's binding of inner and outer would let anger, grief, and a tirade against society reside so fully in eight brief lines?

THE second stance, the reflective, is the most common in current writing. Here, the poet looks at the outer with a steady and questioning eye, neither imposing the self upon it nor disappearing into it; and out of that meeting, something happens, something is learned. A poem that is at one level about the difference between the first stance and the second is Zbigniew Herbert's "Pebble":

The pebble
is a perfect creature

equal to itself
mindful of its limits

filled exactly
with a pebbly meaning

with a scent which does not remind one of anything
does not frighten anything away does not arouse desire

its ardour and coldness
are just and full of dignity

I feel a heavy remorse
when I hold it in my hand
and its noble body
is permeated by false warmth

—Pebbles cannot be tamed
  to the end they will look at us
  with a calm and very clear eye
  (trans. Czeslaw Milosz and Peter Dale Scott)

Herbert instills the pebble with human qualities when he speaks of its ardour and coldness, dignity, mindfulness; he also tells us that it has none, when he speaks of the hand's "false warmth" permeating its "noble body." The point of this poem, which may be read as well as a parable of political resistance, is that a pebble remains in the end wholly itself: beyond corruption, beyond whatever human meaning we may attribute to it—even the poet's. This envoy of the objective becomes a thing we may measure ourselves by safely.

In some reflective poems, the poet observes an outer phenomenon and is reminded of his or her own life, as in this tanka of mourning by Izumi Shikibu, similar in its imagery to another poem of hers seen earlier:

Last year's
fragile, vanished snow
is falling now again—
if only seeing you
could be like this.

The poem's tension comes from its contrast of inner and outer realms. Once again, a death and a snowfall are linked in the poet's mind. Here, the falling snow returns, but the poet's dead lover cannot; her grief infuses and is infused by the coldness and whiteness that take the whole landscape, beyond human will or wishes.

To look at the natural world's recurrences and be reminded of human transience is also the approach of Yeats's "The Wild Swans at Coole":

> The trees are in their autumn beauty,
> The woodland paths are dry,
> Under the October twilight the water
> Mirrors a still sky;
> Upon the brimming water among the stones
> Are nine-and-fifty swans.
>
> The nineteenth autumn has come upon me
> Since I first made my count;
> I saw, before I had well finished,
> All suddenly mount
> And scatter wheeling in great broken rings
> Upon their clamorous wings.
>
> I have looked upon those brilliant creatures,
> And now my heart is sore.
> All's changed since I, hearing at twilight,
> The first time on this shore,
> The bell-beat of their wings above my head,
> Trod with a lighter tread.
>
> Unwearied still, lover by lover,
> They paddle in the cold
> Companionable streams or climb the air;
> Their hearts have not grown old;
> Passion or conquest, wander where they will,
> Attend upon them still.
>
> But now they drift on the still water,
> Mysterious, beautiful;
> Among what rushes will they build,

By what lake's edge or pool
Delight men's eyes when I awake some day
To find they have flown away?

These swans are swans, and more than swans. The poem wavers,
perhaps, between the consciousness of the first stance and that of the
second—as Czeslaw Milosz's "Window" does as well. But Milosz's
apple tree, though real, rests finally in the realm of inner experience,
while Yeats's birds paddle first and last in the seen, whatever migra-
tions of meaning they may have undertaken in between.

A section of Virgil's *Georgics* asks a question inherent to a poem of
the reflective mode—whose reality are we being given?

> The gravid mares
> graze out their months in gentle stateliness,
> freed from all human burdens by their own,
> kept close in care, pastured in shady fields
> where quiet rivers lap the quieter moss
> that lines their banks.
>
> The mares go out at dawn
> and again at dusk (avoiding the gadflies' noon);
> you see them taking shape in the morning mist
>
> or burnished by the golden light of sunset . . .
> Tricks of the light?
>
> But we must believe our eyes
> even at miracles. Huge and yet delicate,
> they stalk their time, the creatures of a dream
> (The gods'? Ours? Their own?).
>
> And wake.
> And foal.
> The marvel of it fades—all marvels do—
> and feeling our way, our confidence again,

we lapse into routines, as the gods do, too,
of the business of life.

(trans. David Slavitt)

The question—in whose dreams do these mares live?—is unanswer-
able. And yet the waking, and the foaling, and the poem-writing,
occur: each a refuge and intermission in the business of everyday
mind.

A last example of a poem of the reflective stance is one that moves
in its thinking toward the objective, Denise Levertov's "Brother Ivy."

Between road and sidewalk, the broadleafed ivy,
unloved, dusty, littered, sanctuary of rats,
gets on with its life. New leaves shine gaily
among dogged older ones
that have lost their polish.
It does not require appreciation. The foliage
conceals a brown tangle of stems
thick as a mangrove swamp; the roots
are spread tenaciously. Unwatered
throughout the long droughts, it simply
grips the dry ground by the scruff of the neck.

I am not its steward.
If we are siblings, and I
my brother's keeper therefore,
the relationship is reciprocal. The ivy
meets its obligation by pure
undoubtable being.

A POETRY of "pure undoubtable being" . . . impossible, surely. The
earth does not speak our language. And yet some poems approach
that state, and many more point toward it. Robinson Jeffers longed
throughout his life to take such a stance, but could not bear to relin-

quish his moral connection with the humanity he continually condemned for its self-centeredness. (He explores the dilemma directly in one late lyric, "On an Anthology of Chinese Poetry.") Czeslaw Milosz points toward it, too, when he writes, "Great was that chase with the hounds for the unattainable meaning of the world." The line is not only moving, but essential: it knows that the chase for comprehension, however endless, is made in the company of hounds, of life-energies other than our own.

Dōgen addressed the relationship between self and other in the search for Buddhist understanding in a famous description: "To study the Way is to study the self, to study the self is to forget the self, to forget the self is to awaken into the ten thousand things." You cannot leap beyond human consciousness without first going through it; but if you gaze deeply enough into being, eventually you will awaken into the company of everything. The thought goes back to the Buddha, who stated at the moment of his enlightenment (which took place outside, under a tree, when he saw the rising morning star), "Now everything and I awaken." Seeing with clarity is not a solitary task, but involves a companionship so intimate it becomes transformation. The idea is not found only in Eastern traditions. The Christian mystic Meister Eckhart wrote, "The more deeply we are our true selves, the less self is in us."

What kinds of poems take this third stance? In the strictest sense very few. What is commonplace in the visual arts—landscapes, animal paintings, still lifes of wheat sheaves and iris or bowls of fruit—is rarely found in poetry, where human concern seems virtually to insist on inserting its presence. Many poems contain passages of purely outer description, but a poem without human occupancy is rare. Perhaps this is not so surprising, considering the difference in the two media: paint's first home is the sensory outer, but language lives in the human mind and heart.

Nonetheless, some poets, especially within the Buddhist and Taoist traditions, have tried to speak the world beyond the self. Haiku in particular may face outward, like these two by Bashō:

The sea grows dark.
Faint calls of passing ducks
are white.

Lightning—
into its darkness,
a night heron calls.

And these, by the nineteenth-century poet Buson:

Spring rain:
the belly of the frog
is not wet.

Evening wind—
the water slaps
the blue heron's legs.

Each of these poems is a pure observation. The reader can try to find in them a statement about some human situation or consciousness, but the result would be a lesser achievement than they are: seventeen-syllable presentations of what is. And yet—as is equally true of a painting of three persimmons, or of a prize Holstein cow—the act of perception cannot be stripped out completely. In selecting the white calls of the ducks, in the manifest knowledge that only the finest rain would leave dry the underbelly of a frog, the poet's mind-trace appears.

Is it necessary for a poem of the objective stance to exclude the human entirely? If the poet's goal, as Bashō stated, is a poem that is neither subjective nor objective, is it possible to imagine a work in which the "I" might exist simply as one more presence, equal with others? Here is a lyric by the Tang dynasty poet Li Po in which the speaker is present but disappears wholly into the nonsubjective by the poem's end. The effect is something like those Chinese mountain landscape-scrolls in which, if you look with care, you discover the tiny figures of two black-robed monks making their way. It has been suggested that the wanderers are there to give the viewer a point of identification, but I have another theory: that we need to include our self-interest as humans before we can pass beyond it and enter freely the ridges and valleys themselves.

I Make My Home in the Mountains

You ask why I live in the mountain forest,
and I smile, and am silent,
and even my soul remains quiet:
it lives in the other world
which no one owns.
The peach trees blossom.
The water flows.

(trans. Sam Hamill)

Another poem that lives beyond subjective and objective is Dōgen's "Poem on the Treasury of the Clear-Seeing Eye." Without the title or any knowledge of Buddhist imagery, the poem could be read simply in terms of its outer image—but it is both that and something else:

Unmoored
in midnight water,
no waves, no wind,
the empty boat
is flooded with moonlight.

This boat is a boat; it is also a picture of the self after realization, empty of concepts. The moonlight is overspilling moonlight, and also the sign of Buddhist enlightenment. Between image and symbol, ordinary rowboat and poet's mind, there is no difference—for a person unmoored from attachment to self, there is no need to anchor this poem as one thing or the other, as both, as neither. It is there to be stepped into along with Dōgen, and rowed away.

The Western tradition, too, has its poems with objective hearts: Rilke's "The Panther"; the work of William Carlos Williams and others who came to the Asian-influenced theories of imagism; the outward-facing eye of D. H. Lawrence's *Birds, Beasts, and Flowers.* Emily Dickinson, that clear observer, found her way to this stance as well: in "A bird came down the walk" the poet is present, but the attention of the poem is firmly on the bird's being, not her own. And no human point is made by the poem's conclusion:

> And he unrolled his feathers
> And rowed him softer home—
>
> Than Oars divide the Ocean,
> Too silver for a seam—
> Or Butterflies, off Banks of Noon
> Leap, plashless as they swim.

▾   ▾   ▾   ▾   ▾

Is THERE some quality in birds—the way their presence among us might be withdrawn at any moment, or the way that part of us follows them into distance and disappears—that causes them to recur so regularly in exploring the issues considered here? Wallace Stevens's "Thirteen Ways of Looking at a Blackbird" is a work as useful as any I know for seeing into poetry's various modes of inward and outward looking. Within its quick succession of images, observations, reflections, and questions, the poem's perspective darts, jinks, and plunges, testing each mode for what revelation it may yield.

I

Among twenty snowy mountains,
The only moving thing
Was the eye of the blackbird.

II

I was of three minds,
Like a tree
In which there are three blackbirds.

III

The blackbird whirled in the autumn winds.
It was a small part of the pantomime.

IV

A man and a woman
Are one.
A man and a woman and a blackbird
Are one.

V

I do not know which to prefer,
The beauty of inflections
Or the beauty of innuendoes,
The blackbird whistling
Or just after.

VI

Icicles filled the long window
With barbaric glass.

The shadow of the blackbird
Crossed it, to and fro.
The mood
Traced in the shadow
An indecipherable cause.

VII

O thin men of Haddam,
Why do you imagine golden birds?
Do you not see how the blackbird
Walks around the feet
Of the women about you?

VIII

I know noble accents
And lucid, inescapable rhythms;
But I know, too,
That the blackbird is involved
In what I know.

IX

When the blackbird flew out of sight,
It marked the edge
Of one of many circles.

X

At the sight of blackbirds
Flying in a green light,
Even the bawds of euphony
Would cry out sharply.

XI

He rode over Connecticut
in a glass coach.
Once, a fear pierced him,
In that he mistook
The shadow of his equipage
For blackbirds.

XII

The river is moving.
The blackbird must be flying.

XIII

It was evening all afternoon.
It was snowing
And it was going to snow.
The blackbird sat
In the cedar-limbs.

Helen Vendler has described the dilemma at the core of Stevens's work as being "whether one reaches the sublime by fleeing the real or by seeking it." Following the blackbird of this poem from stanza to stanza, we can see each of these impulses exerting its attraction. We can also begin to discern how the single image of blackbird, approached through a series of different poetic strategies and points of view, allows Stevens to explore his question more fully. Certain dilemmas cannot be resolved; still, in knowing them better, some purchase on our life is gained.

The poem's first stanza proceeds by straightforward, objective presentation. Much like a haiku in feeling, it leaves the reader to determine for himself what it may mean. The eye of the blackbird might be an image for consciousness; certainly it is what we identify with amid the snow-covered landscape, infinite in its twenty mountains. (Stevens uses "twenty" much as the Chinese use "ten thousand," to hold the multitudinous within the exact.) But because the poem is new at this point, the blackbird is mostly blackbird, the real simply real—and we are satisfied to let it be that.

With the second stanza, a self enters the poem: "I was of three minds." But external image immediately returns: "Like a tree / in which there are three blackbirds." To roost in the outer comes as a relief: being in three minds requires some form of resolution. The psychological theory of cognitive dissonance suggests that the mind in which realities conflict will sacrifice whatever it must to achieve coherence. John Keats, on the other hand, wrote of great poetry's nonsimplifying relationship to complex truth. This verse, then, shows a poet's way out of the psyche's dilemma: three blackbirds in easy accord with the tree that holds them. Still, its portrait of a divided understanding introduces a first hint of Stevens's ambivalence and the complexities to come.

In the third stanza, a blackbird whirls in the autumn winds, first in the realm of simple nature, then, with the word "pantomime," in the realm of the human—a very Stevensian word for our larger situation. Like the blackbird itself, perhaps, the reader is made slightly uneasy, even dizzy, by the perspective. A wind that is pantomime is not wind at all, and the blackbird has been shifted to a new level, suddenly a creature of inner existence. For in this poem, the imagination meets the outer image in a number of different ways: sometimes the object of the poet's attention, at other times the bird is a figure for the poet himself.

The fourth stanza again moves to a different terrain: metaphysics. Its two propositions are couched in the simplest possible language, yet they are rich with implication. The Zen text called the *Sandokai* (The

Meeting of the Many and the One) suggests that within the mind of Oneness, only what is fully separate can also be fully equal. When the blackbird enters the stanza, the oneness of the poem's man and woman changes. Oneness itself changes, becoming unmerged as well as merged. Blackbird, man, and woman stand plainly before the eye, both many and joined.

In the fifth stanza, the first-person speaker reenters the poem, bringing a new question, from the realm of aesthetics: Is the thing itself, or our unspoken response to it, the point? As in the second stanza, the poet presents himself as divided, but now the content of that dilemma begins to come clearer: innuendo takes place in the inner realm, inflection plays itself out in the outer. Here the blackbird may seem to be symbol, a descriptive illustration, but the living bird of the preceding stanzas preens its glossy feathers just offstage. However illustrative, its clear whistling is still heard.

Stanza 6 turns back to outward description, though more complexly; its strategy remains dipped in the symbolic. The window is the window of human vision, distorted by icicles, its growing coldness an intimation of death. The true blackbird, outside and beyond reach, remains an ungraspable knowledge. The portrait here, it seems, is not of the poet either seeking or fleeing the real, but of the elusive real itself: residing not only in the bird, but also in what inner life ("the mood") may radiate back into the world.

The seventh stanza, portraying the choice between the actual and its idealized version living only within the mind, shifts into a second-person address. The blackbird is two-fold: again the common and outer bird, it is also a symbol for the rejected shadow-side of ordinary life. The real bird does not require glamour or even flight to dwell companionably with the women—who, the reader may surmise, are also neglected by these male ascetics who quest for the sublime amid unreal "golden birds." The thought-line continues in the following stanza, but now more subjectively, as the poem returns to first-person speech. Taken together, the two sections of the poem propose that neither art nor ordinary life can be complete without the living black-bird—which is, in the eighth stanza, paradoxically, pure idea.

The ninth stanza offers a tiny metaphysical narrative. The circle it speaks of may be only one among many, but it is nonetheless essen-tial—the circle of what can be known. The blackbird's disappearance from the poem offers a path beyond the range of conscious intellect and will: it dips us into multiplicity, into the realm of Dōgen's unmoored boat.

In the tenth stanza, the departed bird returns: altered by its immer-sion in unknowing, enriched and grown into plurality in the strange light. Perhaps it is the green light that at times flashes up like an other-worldly blessing at sunset, perhaps the light of surreal imagina-tion. The sight overwhelms even those who think they may create or understand the imagination—or worse, own it; these blackbirds mov-ing freely, outside the self, are beyond poetry's control. The real appearing within a halo of the sublime, they startle the reader out of any trained and intellectual confidence, into the pure acknowledg-ment of sensual beauty.

The eleventh stanza brings a self-deprecating third-person por-trait of the poet: a nobleman of artifice, traveling in a vehicle of fragile self-definition. Everything here is idea—even the landscape is named only as a concept, "Connecticut"—and so everything is vulner-able even to a mistaken hint of the untameable real. One strong peck, and such a world shatters.

In stanza 12 the poem returns to descriptive external image to hold its statement; only the subjunctive "must" hints of a subtle human presence. The stanza has the quality of a verse from the *Tao Te Ching*, sure of a truth grounded in nature. When a river acts as a river, the poem proposes, the blackbird must also be free to follow its blackbird course. Inner and outer are again in the accord a good image always offers—but while in the first stanza almost everything was frozen in stasis excepting the single eye of the blackbird, as the poem nears its end, all is in flux. When the imagination is in harmony with a larger whole, both can move.

In the final stanza something mysterious unfolds in the way a human consciousness is quietly at work without declaring itself. The light is defined in human terms, "evening all afternoon," and a thoroughly human awareness of time also suffuses the lines "it was snowing / and it was going to snow." The blackbird is now the one thing at rest in the center of motion; it perches in a cedar that may well be the tree of the second stanza, rooted now in the particular. The cedar stands close to the unmentioned house from whose window the poem's human perspective looks out: an open consciousness that is not trying to exclude, include, or make anything happen. It accepts the ongoing nature of time, of snow, of the real and undefinable bird.

This final vision of the blackbird is much like the one at the poem's beginning. But the journey of the poem has transformed and informed it, just as the many different strategies the poem employs (of objective, subjective, speculative, descriptive, imaginative, and narrative mind) come to inform the intimate and deeply physical observation and speech of the concluding section. The poem ends as it began, in the past tense. Yet still something is present; something is watching. It has neither blessed us nor judged us, but is part of what we know. That is enough.

Stevens wrote in one of his early journals: "I thought, on the train, how utterly we have forsaken the Earth, in the sense of excluding it from our thoughts. There are but few who consider its physical hugeness, its rough enormity. It is still a disparate monstrosity, full of solitudes + barrens + wilds. It still dwarfs + terrifies + crushes. The rivers still roar, the mountains still crash, the winds still shatter. Man is an affair of cities. His gardens + orchards + fields are mere scrapings. Somehow, however, he has managed to shut out the face of the giant from his windows. But the giant is there, nevertheless." The blackbird beyond the window—in the mountains, in the psyche, in the snowy tree —is one face of that giant, silently asking our attention.

IN THINKING about the relationship of inner and outer in the making of poetic meaning, there is one more work I would like to consider—*The Tempest*. The play is about forgiveness, but also about the setting-right of one man's relationship to nature. It is Prospero's desire for an unnatural enchantment that cost him his dukedom; throughout the long years of his exile and slow maturation he never doubts his right to control both Ariel, spirit of air and aesthetic beauty, and Caliban, spirit of all things earthy and subterranean, whose labor sustains his master and mistress's daily and animal life. The speech that ends with Prospero's vow to drown his book still holds a faint, lingering echo of the thrill he took in his old domination of sea and wind, of spirit and trees.

Such a relationship to nature is endlessly tempting. But if Prospero is to step into his proper powers and responsibilities, he must first give up this misguided magic and set its spirits free. Prospero cannot be fully Prospero until Ariel and Caliban also become fully themselves, undeflected by his human consciousness and desires. Then, when in the epilogue the old magus declares, "What strength I have's mine own," the hearer recognizes the great rightness in his statement: in reassuming worldly power as a duke, Prospero also steps once more into vulnerability. He is now at the mercy of the community at large— human, animal, mineral, spiritual—and must humbly ask its assistance to continue on his path.

In this act lies the second secret of this chapter's title. Good poetry begins with seeing increasingly clearly, in increasingly various ways;

but another part of poetry's true perception is found only in relinquishing more and more of the self to more and more of the world. I do not know any prescription for doing this. It may be that the world does it for us, and to us, however the writer may struggle and resist. Life in its joy and grief and boredom and richness instructs us in the passage from infant's experience of world-as-entirely-self toward the ripeness we find in the late work of a few writers and artists. We find over and over again in their mature pieces the murmur of "Look—marvelous, marvelous . . ." Then even that is swallowed up in the larger chorus.

Facing the Lion: The Way of Shadow and Light in Some Twentieth-Century Poems

▼　▼　▼　▼　▼　▼　▼　▼　▼

STEVIE SMITH once wrote that every poem could be titled either "Heaven, a Detail" or "Hell, a Detail." Every poem is also about the relationship between the two—about the ways the poetry of heaven and the poetry of hell speak to one another and require one another; about the way what transpires between the realm sometimes called shadow and the realm sometimes called light ripens us—as human beings, as readers, as writers—into a more fully realized aliveness. How does this connection work? A good entrance into the question is Yeats's "The Choice":

> The intellect of man is forced to choose
> Perfection of the life, or of the work,
> And if it take the second must refuse
> A heavenly mansion, raging in the dark.
> When all that story's finished, what's the news?
> In luck or out the toil has left its mark:
> That old perplexity an empty purse
> Or the day's vanity, the night's remorse.

At first reading, "The Choice" offers the familiar tale of the artist alone in his or her tiny garret, forgoing ordinary happiness in the ways the life of art so often requires. But there is another way to read the poem, and a second knowledge to be taken from it: if you want to pursue the perfection of the work, this other reading suggests, you must refuse beauty, refuse paradise and ease, and be willing to enter the life of "raging in the dark." This interpretation may well be more than Yeats intended; still, its wisdom is undeniable. It begins to chart a course for what a person must do to cultivate a matured vision.

In the twentieth century especially, artists have taken on the task of exploring that part of human experience C. G. Jung called the shadow. They have consistently endeavored to look at what is difficult to see; to press, by means of both subject matter and new formal techniques, into the realms of sorrow, chaos, indeterminacy, anger; to seek out the places where madness and imagination meet. Shadow plays no larger role in contemporary life than it did in the past—but out of the trenches of World War I a new awareness emerged of such forces *as* shadow, as an uncontrollable thing unleashing itself into the world. Flaring from the poems of Wilfred Owen and, later, from Picasso's *Guernica* is a changed understanding of how utterly war fragments the human spirit. Modern consciousness no longer conceives of a noble cause that is not haunted, nor of a beauty that is not also terrifying. We have learned that every gift carries its price.

The knowledge, though never so explicitly articulated, is not new. It goes back at least to Dante, whose journey to Paradise, as we have already seen, begins with the descent into Hell. Opening with the loss of both way and self to fear and despair, it proceeds according to the Heraclitean rule that the way up is the way down. The poet's path to integration passes through limbo, through icy despair, through realms of terror and pain; and while the guiding figure of Virgil warns him against identifying too closely with those he meets, Dante must nonetheless take in their existence with his full and unwavering gaze.

Earlier still is the Greek myth of Prometheus, condemned to spend eternity chained to the top of a mountain, his liver torn by vultures, after bringing to humankind the gift of fire: what lights our darkness bears a terrible cost. The Egyptian story of Osiris and its many variations speak of a necessary descent into dismemberment or death before the return to a life no longer experienced as innocent or guaranteed, but as cyclical, bargained for, and only provisionally won back. Finally, there is the story of Eve, whose illicit desire for knowledge unleashes upon herself and her descendants the myriad sufferings of birth and death and existence subject to time.

Everywhere we look, the theme appears: wisdom, at least in the West, is obtained through transgression and paid for in suffering. The journey into maturity, whether seen in Odysseus or Aeneas or the joined figures of Persephone and Demeter, must pass through the underworld realms of uncertainty, fear, and death, before the green and peaceful life the hero longs for can be restored—and both world and self are irrevocably changed by that immersion. Deception, too, has its role in each of these stories. Craftiness and trickery are a part of the test—we are tricked into falling, and tricked into wisdom. It is worth pausing to note the word, *craftiness:* the beauty of art—its craft—is a conjury, a sleight of hand enacted against dullness, inattention, ignorance, and the inner and outer faces of death.

Eastern traditions show a less consistent linkage between shadow and knowledge. Still, in one of the Jataka stories (traditional Indian folktales about the past lives of the Buddha), the Buddha, finding himself on a mountain ledge above a starving tigress and her ravenous cubs, throws himself into her jaws in order to save her life. In this case, it is in the service of a different kind of ripening—the development of a limitless, selfless compassion—that the descent into death is required. Still, the story seems woven of kindred thread.

▾   ▾   ▾   ▾   ▾

MORE poems touch on the image of giving oneself to the lion and the tiger than one might guess. One rather odd example is a poem by Stevie Smith:

The Photograph

They photographed me young upon a tiger skin
And now I do not care at all for kith and kin,
For oh the tiger nature works within.

Parents of England, not in smug
Fashion fancy set on rug
Of animal fur the darling you would hug,

For lately born is not too young
To scent the savage he sits upon,
And tiger-possessed abandon all things human.

The poem suggests that what creates an artist (which means, at least in part, a person whose life is dedicated to the developing process, as a photograph is) is exposure to the tiger, for even the briefest of moments. A parent may think she or he is choosing only a decorative background for a baby picture, the poem warns, but will end up with a child devoured. After this first contact, nothing will keep the tiger nature suppressed—a savage pursuit of truth becomes more important than kindness, than connection, than any ties. Parents do not want their children to become artists because they know this. They fear not only for the child's outer well-being (remember Yeats's prediction that the artist will most likely end up with an empty purse), but also the havoc that the pursuit of art will wreak, not just upon the child's inner life, but upon themselves. A savage spirit raging in the dark does not sit lightly and easily through Thanksgiving dinners; it refuses to charm, to acquiesce, to go to bed at a reasonable hour, to bend to the ways of the world. Even the poem's prosody echoes the statement, as the regular rhymes of the first two stanzas give way to the less-tamed calling of sound to sound in "young," "upon," and "human." A freedom has entered in, and the poet can do what she wishes.

A longer poem on the subject is Allen Ginsberg's "The Lion for Real":

The Lion for Real
   Soyez muette pour moi, Idole contemplative . . .

I came home and found a lion in my living room
Rushed out on the fire-escape screaming Lion! Lion!
Two stenographers pulled their brunette hair and banged the
       window shut
I hurried home to Paterson and stayed two days.

Called up my old Reichian analyst
who'd kicked me out of therapy for smoking marijuana
"It's happened" I panted "There's a Lion in my room"
"I'm afraid any discussion would have no value" he hung up.

I went to my old boyfriend we got drunk with his girlfriend
I kissed him and announced I had a lion with a mad gleam in my eye
We wound up fighting on the floor I bit his eyebrow and he kicked
       me out
I ended masturbating in his jeep parked in the street moaning
       "Lion."

Found Joey my novelist friend and roared at him "Lion!"
He looked at me interested and read me his spontaneous ignu high
       poetries
I listened for lions all I heard was Elephant Tiglon Hippogriff
       Unicorn Ants
But figured he really understood me when we made it in Ignaz
       Wisdom's bathroom.

But next day he sent me a leaf from his Smoky Mountain retreat
"I love you little Bo-Bo with your delicate golden lions
But there being no Self and No Bars therefore the Zoo of your dear
     Father hath no Lion
You said your mother was mad don't expect me to produce the
     Monster for your Bridegroom."

Confused dazed and exalted bethought me of real lion starved in his
     stink in Harlem
Opened the door the room was filled with the bomb blast of his
     anger
He roaring hungrily at the plaster walls but nobody could hear him
     outside thru the window
My eye caught the edge of the red neighbor apartment building
     standing in deafening stillness

We gazed at each other his implacable yellow eye in the red halo
     of fur
Waxed rheumy on my own but he stopped roaring and bared a fang
     greeting.
I turned my back and cooked broccoli for supper on an iron gas stove
boilt water and took a hot bath in the old tub under the sink board.

He didn't eat me, tho I regretted him starving in my presence.
Next week he wasted away a sick rug full of bones wheaten hair
     falling out
enraged and reddening eye as he lay aching huge hairy head on
     his paws
by the egg-crate bookcase filled up with thin volumes of Plato, &
     Buddha.

Sat by his side every night averting my eyes from his hungry
     motheaten face
Stopped eating myself he got weaker and roared at night while I
     had nightmares

Eaten by lion in bookstore on Cosmic Campus, a lion myself starved
    by Professor Kandinsky, dying in a lion's flophouse circus,
I woke up mornings the lion still added dying on the floor—"Terrible
    Presence!" I cried "Eat me or die!"

It got up that afternoon—walked to the door with its paw on the wall
    to steady its trembling body
Let out a soul rending creak from the bottomless roof of his mouth
Thundering from my floor to heaven heavier than a volcano at night
    in Mexico
Pushed the door open and said in a gravelly voice "Not this time
    Baby—but I will be back again."

Lion that eats my mind now for a decade knowing only your hunger
Not the bliss of your satisfaction O roar of the Universe how am I
    chosen
In this life I have heard your promise I am ready to die I have served
Your starved and ancient Presence O Lord I wait in my room at your
    Mercy.

The whole story is here. The lion enters, we run away, we try everything to distract ourselves, our friends don't believe what we tell them . . . then, the unavoidable battle of wills, the surrender. And more—to be rejected still, forced into a continuing precarious existence that must be deepened and further deepened before the vow is accepted. For giving oneself to the lion, or to poetry, is a vow—nothing more, nothing less than one's entire life will be asked.

The poem clarifies something: the lion is not simply the id. Sex, hunger, dreams—none of these is "the lion for real." They are what Ginsberg turns to in his various attempts to face or not face the lion. The lion-for-real is a being far more complex, more multidimensional, and more outer. Not simply some untamed part of the self, it is an untamed part of the world, something that cannot be owned or controlled, that must in the end be acknowledged because its presence in our lives is irrefutable, overwhelming, and—if we allow it to be—transformative.

A first impulse is to think that giving oneself to the lion is a matter of simple courage—and to some extent it is. To write is to open one's door to what chooses to knock, not knowing whether one will meet the disguised god or the disguised demon of so many traditional tales. Either visitation bears gifts. But courage alone will not suffice: remember that Ginsberg doesn't—can't—get away with a single flamboyant gesture. Doggedness better describes the spirit with which he moves back into his apartment, resumes the activities of daily life, cooks broccoli, bathes. Much of the time, it seems, he can't even look at the presence he's living with. But neither can he leave it: "Sat by his side every night averting my eyes from his hungry motheaten face," the poem says. It is the way that the ancient Greeks knew the god of the underworld, Hades. In numerous vase paintings, his image appears looking away—not only because it is impossible for the living to meet directly the gaze of death, but also because a hiddenness lies at death's core.

The trick, then, is to let the lion into the house without abandoning one's allegiance to the world of the living: to live amid the overpowering scent of its knowledge, yet not be dragged entirely into its realm. This is the reason Dante is forbidden pity when he looks upon the damned—to feel their fate too intimately would put his own salvation at risk. What is required is a certain distance—made, in part, through the mind of art itself. Every poet is a Scheherazade, acceding to fate while at the same time delaying it. And Scheherazade's salvation, not unlike Dante's, is accomplished by abundance and imagination, by her offering the cruel king the one thing he cannot do without: a story worth hearing. For it is not our death the lion wants to eat, but our lives. In the difference lies one of the great source-springs of poetic power.

FAILURE is also possible: Rilke's "The Panther" describes what happens when the vow is refused. The great black cat pacing ceaselessly behind the bars of the Paris zoological garden comes finally to a numbness into which the entire world disappears. This is the fate of the human spirit as well, if it tries to make of the untameable a thing wholly caged.

The Panther
   In the Jardin des Plantes, Paris

His vision, from the constantly passing bars,
has grown so weary that it cannot hold
anything else. It seems to him there are
a thousand bars; and behind the bars, no world.

As he paces in cramped circles, over and over,
the movement of his powerful soft strides
is like a ritual dance around a center
in which a mighty will stands paralyzed.

Only at times, the curtain of the pupils
lifts, quietly—. An image enters in,
rushes down through the tensed, arrested muscles,
plunges into the heart and is gone.

                                    (trans. Stephen Mitchell)

Still another danger lies not in refusal of the lion's nature, but in putting oneself too easily into its mouth, forgetting to love also the infinite stories of the world. This kind of surrender might explain the strange blossoming of serenity in Sylvia Plath's last poems. One, "Edge," begins:

The woman is perfected.
Her dead

Body wears the smile of accomplishment,
The illusion of a Greek necessity

Flows in the scrolls of her toga,
Her bare

Feet seem to be saying:
We have come this far, it is over . . .

Perfection for Plath (of the life? of the work?) is the vision of her
own body composed in death, her two children coiled by her breasts,
which the poem's measured voice unfolds as quietly and inexorably as
a ticking clock. And see how the more propulsive "Ariel"—whose title
refers not to the sprite of *The Tempest* but to Plath's horse, named after
that spirit—describes the fierce being whose gallop leads her away
from the world's claims and toward a driving, suicidal union: "God's
lioness."

IN THE face of sufficient pain, surrender is an understandable choice.
But another poem of riding toward death comes to mind, in tempera-
ment more akin to Allen Ginsberg's—"The Abnormal Is Not Cour-
age," by Jack Gilbert:

The Poles rode out from Warsaw against the German
tanks on horses. Rode knowing, in sunlight, with sabers.
A magnitude of beauty that allows me no peace.
And yet this poem would lessen that day. Question
the bravery. Say it's not courage. Call it a passion.
Would say courage isn't that. Not at its best.
It was impossible, and with form. They rode in sunlight.
Were mangled. But I say courage is not the abnormal.
Not the marvelous act. Not Macbeth with fine speeches.
The worthless can manage in public, or for the moment.
It is too near the whore's heart: the bounty of impulse,
and the failure to sustain even small kindness.

Not the marvelous act, but the evident conclusion of being.
Not strangeness, but a leap forward of the same quality.
Accomplishment. The even loyalty. But fresh.
Not the Prodigal Son, nor Faustus. But Penelope.
The thing steady and clear. Then the crescendo.
The real form. The culmination. And the exceeding.
Not the surprise. The amazed understanding. The marriage,
not the month's rapture. Not the exception. The beauty
that is of many days. Steady and clear.
It is the normal excellence, of long accomplishment.

To live fully and willingly in the world of the living is more brave even than going open-eyed toward death. All too often we do neither, and, clinging to some safer middle ground, end by feeling neither our terrors nor our joys. But one of the laws of poetry is that no good poem can be wholly safe or wholly pure. A good poem's blessings are mixed, as love poems, for example, live best in the knowledge of love's transience. It is also a law of the self: "Every angel is terrifying," Rilke wrote. If a poem would describe joy, it seems it must also hold joy's shadow.

To see how this works, here is a poem that seems at first to describe a moment of pure light, pure redemption, by Czeslaw Milosz:

Gift

A day so happy.
Fog lifted early, I worked in the garden.
Hummingbirds were stopping over honeysuckle flowers.
There was no thing on earth I wanted to possess.
I knew no one worth my envying him.
Whatever evil I had suffered, I forgot.
To think that once I was the same man did not embarrass me.
In my body I felt no pain.
When straightening up, I saw the blue sea and sails.

(trans. Czeslaw Milosz)

Because we feel immediately that this is a good poem, we know it must have somewhere within it the shadow of a lion, who may be mostly hidden, but is nonetheless present. The prestidigitation is done, I think, in two ways. The first is that each outward object in the poem embodies transience—what is more ephemeral than lifting fog, more quick than the unmentioned wings of the hummingbirds stopped above their flowers? Blue seas alter in a moment, raised sails by definition pass us by. Reading the deep poem underlying the poem at first apparent, we recognize the loveliness of the entire scene as only an instant's reprieve from temporality. The second part of the trick is the rhetorical device of including a thing by putting it in the negative. Evil, suffering, physical pain, shame, the desire to possess—by telling us that for this moment each was forgotten, the poet makes us feel their presence pressing in all around this moment. This surrounding landscape of difficulty gives the poem's one day of peace its poignance. The title contributes as well: a gift is unearned, unpurchasable, and so also a thing that cannot be controlled. In that thought, too, lies the undomesticated footprint of the lion.

In much the same way, an effective strategy for presenting horror is to turn to horror's shadow-side: to the fragile yet persistent beauty of the world. Consider Frost's chilling war-sonnet, "Range-Finding":

The battle rent a cobweb diamond-strung
And cut a flower beside a ground bird's nest
Before it stained a single human breast.
The stricken flower bent double and so hung.
And still the bird revisited her young.
A butterfly its fall had dispossessed
A moment sought in air his flower of rest,
Then lightly stooped to it and fluttering clung.

On the bare upland pasture there had spread
O'ernight 'twixt mullein stalks a wheel of thread

And straining cables wet with silver dew.
A sudden passing bullet shook it dry.
The indwelling spider ran to greet the fly,
But finding nothing, sullenly withdrew.

The rhetoric of inclusion by denial is taken here to the next degree.
The true subject of the poet's concern goes almost unmentioned—
and the poem, I think, would be even better if Frost had trusted his
readers enough to leave out the third line ("Before it stained a single
human breast"). The title is sufficient hint for "Range-Finding" to
make its point, a point chilling precisely because at the poem's close
the bent flower still holds its butterfly, the nestlings still live; even the
shaken spiderweb is intact. Reciting the litany of fragile things that
survive the setting of the guns' scopes, Frost leaves the reader to imag-
ine everything else. And the fly of the final couplet, whose mention
carries all the resonance of carrion death—fly as food for spider; fly as
what will remain, feasting on, when the battle ends—is itself an
absence, a mistaken idea of the spider whose web has been brushed.
This poem is a tour de force, its substance kept almost entirely in
shadow.

The withheld carries great power. In *The Open Door*, theater direc-
tor Peter Brook praises empty space as the stage set in which an audi-
ence's imagination can reach its highest engagement; he writes also
that actors' true presence appears only when they have entered an
inner silence. The description recalls the *hana*, or "flower," of Zeami's
Nō, through which an actor can move his audience even when stand-
ing motionless and masked on a mostly bare stage. In youth, Zeami
writes, such *hana* may appear naturally, but in age it requires a person
thoroughly ripened. That mature *hana* is the reflection of secret
knowledge, a thing unexpressed: the great actor knows more than he
shows. Yet Zeami cautions that even the fact that the actor possesses a
secret should be kept secret. He describes *hana* with a traditional Zen

phrase: just like "the light of the sun at midnight," it is felt most deeply when unseen.

Certain poems, like Milosz's "Gift," have this quality as well. In even the simplest of such poems, complexity hovers: sign of a consciousness developed by long consideration, long encounter with the blunt and delicate forces of existence. Such poems have a shadow because they have being and substance, an inescapable sense of history within which they see what they know and convey it to us. Such poems know more than they tell. They keep secrets. Yet that unspoken knowledge shapes and flavors and alchemizes all that is said.

▾   ▾   ▾   ▾   ▾

THERE is shadow in poetry in the specifically Jungian sense as well: those aspects of the self which most discomfort. How often some new biography is published and the reader finds herself baffled: how is it that poems so loved and admired could have been written by a person so deeply, cruelly flawed? The question is raised by the misogyny and bigotry of Larkin's letters, by Stevens's racism, by Pound's and Eliot's anti-Semitism, by the cruelty and carelessness toward others that mark the stories of many recent poets. These flaws are not necessarily unconscious. Commenting to Kingsley Amis, Larkin once wrote, "I have always taken comfort from D. H. L[awrence]'s 'You have to have something vicious in you to be a creative writer.'"

Yet it may be that the bitterness, vanity, selfishness, and fear that to some degree inhabit each of us may also bring the shadow's complex gifts into the work of a poet forced to struggle particularly hard against them. Perhaps a cruel eye, if kept in check well enough by the demands of making good art, may make—at least at times—for a better poet than a lazy eye or a stupid or sleeping one, or one that willingly blinds itself to the more harsh aspects of the world and the human. A poem that struggles against its own bitterness may seem gallant; one that struggles against the saccharin will be merely pitiful. Kay Ryan has observed, "It's as if such poets are holding a knife by the blade while they write." In the attempt to cut neither the reader nor themselves, an astonishing tenderness may emerge.

For there is no question that the best of Larkin's poems move finally toward tenderness, born perhaps out of knowing the wound of a sharp judgment turned as quickly upon himself as upon others. In his most achieved work, as soon as the blade-edge of judgment and bitterness rises, Larkin widens the perspective, includes himself, and the poem steps into a larger knowledge and compassion. The gesture is clearly at work in "High Windows."

High Windows

When I see a couple of kids
And guess he's fucking her and she's
Taking pills or wearing a diaphragm,
I know this is paradise

Everyone old has dreamed of all their lives—
Bonds and gestures pushed to one side
Like an outdated combine harvester,
And everyone young going down the long slide

To happiness, endlessly. I wonder if
Anyone looked at me, forty years back,
And thought, *That'll be the life;*
No God anymore, or sweating in the dark

About hell and that, or having to hide
What you think of the priest. He
And his lot will all go down the long slide
Like free bloody birds. And immediately

Rather than words comes the thought of high windows:
The sun-comprehending glass,
And beyond it, the deep blue air, that shows
Nothing, and is nowhere, and is endless.

The poem is woven seamlessly of voice and idea and image and sound. A long *i* guides the reader from the "I" and "paradise" of the first stanza through "lives," "pushed to one side," "long slide," and "hide," to the last stanza's return to the "high windows" first heard in the title. Similarly, there is the end-sound of "happiness": first met at the base of that initial long slide, it recurs altered and opened and freed of bitterness in the "sun-comprehending glass" and "endless" of the poem's conclusion. The unspoken word, filling that empty blue depth, is "blessing." There's no missing the bitterness Larkin feels about his own disordered sex life and lost chances; still, in thought and music, the poem moves from its first anger to something completely mysterious, the openness to light and air with which it ends.

That shift is a point of craft that cannot be learned except in the heart itself—it can't be faked or cobbled together the way a good simile sometimes can. A person may learn it from his or her own life, or possibly from reading, but an essential part of a poet's ripening into tenderness entails not excusing himself anymore. Larkin at his best doesn't let Larkin at his worst off the hook, nor does he avoid Larkin at his worst. He does the one thing he is able to do: he lives with himself as best he can, and looks at it all.

The ability to hold the worse parts of the self subject to examination and judgment may also redeem Robert Lowell from, for example, the utter selfishness of the sonnets he wrote about the end of his marriage to Elizabeth Hardwick. Here is one poem that shows the process at work:

Dolphin

My Dolphin, you only guide me by surprise,
captive as Racine, the man of craft,
drawn through his maze of iron composition
by the incomparable wandering voice of Phèdre.
When I was troubled in mind, you made for my body
caught in its hangman's-knot of sinking lines,
the glassy bowing and scraping of my will . . .
I have sat and listened to too many
words of the collaborating muse,
and plotted perhaps too freely with my life,
not avoiding injury to others,
not avoiding injury to myself—
to ask compassion . . . this book, half fiction,
an eelnet made by man for the eel fighting—

my eyes have seen what my hand did.

The imagery here goes back to Lowell's youth—in his first book, "The Quaker Graveyard in Nantucket" opens with the image of a drowned sailor clutching a drag-net and closes with the line, "The Lord survives the rainbow of his will." A lifetime later, the poet is still working the same vein of ore, still pondering the body drowned in the web of the world and how it got there. By the very act of admitting both his complicity and his unworthiness to ask forgiveness, he wins what he knows he cannot demand: the reader's compassion, and pity even, for his cruelty.

▾   ▾   ▾   ▾   ▾

IN CATHOLIC mysticism there is a path known as the *via negativa*—the practice of emptying the self of its own will, desires, and even knowledge, in order that the soul may be filled by God. Poetry offers a similar path, rich with nondoing. It is found first in the relationship between speech and its steady companion and shadow-side, silence. Silence's abyss holds our utter inadequacy to the task of marrying world and words; holds as well those demons who thrive always amid the unknown. Like a medieval mapmaker, the mind writes over unworded places, "In this place there be dragons."

Yet silence, as we have seen, is birthbed as well as deathbed to meaning, the precursor and necessary ground for all concentrated speech. It removes the mind from the thought-stream of the quotidian, turning it toward the wellspring from which original thought may rise. And so the rituals of silent preparation: Flaubert's drawer of rotting apples was a kind of wordless offering; his opening it each morning was a vow preceding speech, plunging him into a different realm of mind. To step into that uncharted terrain as yet without words is the only way we begin to name the real and not the received.

A closely related step on poetry's via negativa is Keats's famous conception of Negative Capability: the ability of the writer to abide in the realm of mystery and uncertainty, free of any "irritable reaching after facts." A poet's character, Keats wrote, "is not itself—it has no self—it is every thing and nothing—." Using language that comes straight from the mystics, he described the self as being "annihilated" by all that presses in around it. The writer following this path gives himself over to the imagination and its works. Giving up self-preservation, he begins to be able to serve.

Yet another "negative way" in poetry is the literal use of the negative, as seen in Milosz's "Gift." Explicit negative constructions appear in poetry with surprising frequency, often just at that turning point when a poem moves into its subject with new and deeper force. Grammar itself moves the poem into the realm of shadow, syntax seeking what unexpected wisdom that place of not-knowing may bring.

One of the great practitioners of this use of the negative is James Wright, who is also among the most luminous poets of this century. In his later work, filled with an unsurpassed tenderness and compassion, such phrases recur with enormous frequency. Open at random the posthumous collection *This Journey,* published two years after Wright's death in 1980, and you may find, as I did in writing this piece, a poem about Saint Jerome.

Wright's poetic engagement with saints goes back at least to his second book, *Saint Judas.* Jerome lived from roughly 342 to 420; he was not only sainted but also given a rarer title, "doctor of the church," for his work as both theologian and translator. After many years of passionate engagement in church affairs, he retired to a desert monastic community near Bethlehem, where he completed a translation of the Old Testament from Hebrew. It is during this time of respite, late in his life, that Wright's poem is set.

Jerome in Solitude

To see the lizard there,
I was amazed I did not have to beat
My breast with a stone.

If a lion lounged nearby,
He must have curled in a shadow of cypress,
For nobody shook a snarled mane and stretched out
To lie at my feet.

And, for a moment,
I did not see Christ retching in pain, longing
To clutch his cold abdomen,
Sagging, unable to rise or fall, the human
Flesh torn between air and air.

I was not even
Praying, unless: no,
I was not praying.

A rust branch fell suddenly
Down from a dead cypress
And blazed gold. I leaned close.
The deep place in the lizard's eye
Looked back into me.

Delicate green sheaths
Folded into one another.
The lizard was alive,
Happy to move.

But he did not move.
Neither did I.
I did not dare to.

I truly did open the book at random. I did not look for a poem with
a lion in it—yet there one is, present through the strategy of claiming
his absence. Companion-animal of Saint Jerome, the lion traditionally
appears in paintings at the saint's feet while Jerome leans over
his translator's desk. In this poem, the animal appears "curled in a
shadow." From that place of peaceable acknowledgment, he blesses
the poem, the saint, the reader, the poet.

Each of the first four stanzas progresses by means of a statement
made in the negative. "I did not have to beat / My breast with a
stone." "Nobody shook a snarled mane and stretched out / To lie at my
feet." "And for a moment, / I did not see Christ retching in pain, long-
ing / to clutch his cold abdomen." How powerfully this particular use
of the negative allows the image that follows it to enter us—by pre-
tending to release us from the vision of Christ's all-too-human agony,
Wright in fact includes us in it. And finally, "I was not even / Praying,

unless: no, / I was not praying": a negative statement, the reconsidering pause, then the repetition, even more definitive. And yet, instead of closing the poem down, the gesture opens it for the moment of the psyche's deepening and epiphany: for the blazing gold of what at first appears to be a fallen branch, for the "deep place in the lizard's eye" looking back into the poet. The poem's lizard is small and seemingly inconsequential—virtually all James Wright's messenger angels are. Yet his mere being is a gate, entered not by suffering but as the pure gift that comes when we are doing nothing, if we are doing nothing deeply enough.

It is a reenactment, changed and deepened, of Wright's earlier "Saint Judas." In that sonnet Judas, going off to kill himself after the crucifixion, is stopped by the sight of a man being beaten by hoodlums. He drops the rope with which he intends to hang himself, and runs unthinkingly and without any consciousness of self to the victim "beaten, / Stripped, kneed, and left to cry."

> Then I remembered bread my flesh had eaten,
> The kiss that ate my flesh. Flayed without hope,
> I held the man for nothing in my arms.

Only in that nothing can a gift be given or received. Through dark poem after dark poem, Wright pursues that nothing, the state when a person passes beyond valuation and evaluation and becomes only himself. It is the grail that led Wright from the bitter residues of his Depression-era childhood and early breakdown and subsequent alcoholism to the intimate empathy and—there is no other word for it—grace of the late work. Throughout his life as a writer he told of lost souls, of the ones fallen into the river and destroyed. Throughout his life as a writer he was willing to step from safety into those places of raging in the dark. And still we find him at the end of "Jerome in Solitude"—a poem that, whether consciously or unconsciously, must be self-portrait—in a moment of pure suspension, deep in the great happiness of being alive in the saint, in the delicate green folds of the lizard's skin, in the held breath of amazement at the existence of life itself. Surely there is a connection.

"GIFT" and "Jerome in Solitude" show us a grace both embedded in and removed from the flux of world and time, and I do not think it an accident that both poems use what I am calling the "negative way" to achieve their separate miracles. These are rare poems, poems that manage to realize for us an image, however precarious and fleeting, of what Yeats's heavenly mansion looks like. It looks like sailboats on blue water; it looks like the eye of a lizard. Yet the only path to such a poem is the willingness to include its opposite, to live for as long as is necessary in silence, in patience, in raging in the dark—not attempting to turn away, not attempting to exclude the difficult parts of our knowledge of what the world is.

I will finish, then, by returning to Lowell's "Dolphin," a poem caught on the verge of grace. The poem shows how a person moves clumsily, awkwardly, unmusically, apologetically, toward a grace only guessed at, in words that do not flow easily from the tongue but pause, stumble, grope. The dolphin—Lowell's version of the untameable spirit-animal of redemption—will come, if it comes, not by any act the poet can control but only by surprise and as gift, to rescue a man who knows himself drowning in a net of his own construction, result of his human and fallible will. "My eyes have seen what my hand did," the poet concludes, neither excusing nor blaming. This extra, fifteenth line of the sonnet is not only acknowledgment, not only description. It also offers a possible direction: here is a course we can attempt, in our own clumsy navigation of the shadow in world and in self.

We cannot control the dolphin, or the lion, or the gift that comes as a single day of grace. We cannot choose whether or not we will be ready to throw ourselves over the ledge to where the starving tiger looks up. What we can do is be willing to see what we do, what we are, what is around us, and to stake a claim in the marriage of artistic craft to that unflinching and steadfast looking. We can ask for the truth. We can approach it from every side: above, below, backward. We can follow our obsessions and images over the course of a lifetime, returning and returning to the body knotted in its hangman's ropes in the sea at the center of our grief.

Yeats's choice, I think, is a false dichotomy. Raging in the dark is the road to the heavenly mansion, whether in the work or in the life. We have the task clearly before us. Lowell named it elsewhere, in a line I have come to value in a way free of the circumstances of its writing—"Why not say what happened?" If the thought is interpreted deeply and widely enough, with freedom and grace; if we are willing to live with the lion, the tiger, the wild and unbeckonable dolphin— something unknowable may come of such a path, of its suffering that is also blessing. Such a path, chosen fully in all of its junctures, will do.

Poetry as a Vessel of Remembrance

▾   ▾   ▾   ▾   ▾   ▾   ▾   ▾   ▾   ▾

T HE STORY of poetry has many beginnings. One is in Mnemosyne—Remembrance—earliest-born of the Greek goddesses, mother of the Muses and so also of the poem. Hesiod calls her the goddess of the first hour, as it would have to be: at the moment that time appears in the world, change appears in the world, and change alone, lacking memory's steadying counterweight, would mean Chaos. Without the power of memory as Mnemosyne manifests it—creative, flowing ceaselessly from the source of what is— what would connect each moment to the next? Through Mnemosyne, the knowable world continues from moment to moment, and through the poetry she engendered, words first learned to transcend time.

Reading and writing come late. First there is Mnemosyne's world, the oral world whose immense shadow we can see in the works of Homer and which lives on in virtually every characteristic by which we recognize poetry as poetry—all the qualities that work to hold language in place in time. For words themselves are vessels of consciousness, but before the coming of letters placed into clay tablet, papyrus, or book, verbal thought could live only in the fragile containers of inner contemplation and spoken language. Verse, at its most fundamental, is language put into the forms of remembrance. The earliest vessel for holding consciousness that has lasted, poetry is the progenitor of all the technologies of memory to come.

In Mnemosyne's time, memory was not yet imagined as a book or a storage room into which one could look. It was a being who spoke, and the way she spoke was in shapeliness, in verse. When poetry came later to be housed in the material realm of symbol and ink, how and why it was used changed, many of its means changed—but the fundamental sound of Mnemosyne's speech continued to permeate its nature, as does some echo, however faint, of her absolutely central place in human life.

To see how the requirements of memorability created poetry, we need first to imagine the nature of language and knowledge in a purely oral world. As a number of scholars have pointed out, before literacy, sound, not sight, is the sense-realm in which words exist. Perhaps the most striking difference between these two senses is their differing relationships to time. The visual world holds still through time—an oak tree or rock seen yesterday will remain to be seen tomorrow. Or if what we look at moves, we can follow that movement, or at least trust that the thing we have seen could still be found; one of the early, hard-earned lessons of infancy is that what goes out of sight does not cease to exist. Similarly, the written word—language placed into the realm of sight—remains stable over time, staying faithfully, reliably, in its place. Set down in a book, on a shelf, it can be readily returned to hand and mind when needed.

Sound and the spoken word are different: the most fleeting of forms, existing only within the tenuous, present-moment decanting of breath. By the time we hear the last syllable of "moment," the first syllable has already vanished. The knowledge-realm of sound is so immediate that we dare not close it out even for an instant—our ears have no lids, no lips to seal shut. And further, sound is a sense not only of immediate time, but also of physical presence, of connection in space. Human vision divides. Depending as it does on the clear perception of boundaries, it creates a feeling of the outer as opposed to the self, of distinct and separate being. We say, and feel, that we look "out": from the center of our being, vision travels away from us and into the world. But a sound is perceived as coming toward and entering into us, bringing the outer within: sound lives in the movement of our own inner bones joining the resonance of its prior source. It is sound, not light, that summons us almost irresistibly to the linked celebration that is dance. Enveloping and seamless, sound—like taste, like smell—is intimate by its very nature. Yet, like taste, like smell, sound unshaped by human artistry is hard to recall with precision. It lives and vanishes in the instant of its presence.

What is heard—the cry of a child, the fall of a cougar's foot in dry leaves—is always the sign of something changing: only something active makes a noise. In an oral world, the word is indistinguishable from action itself, and so the world of speech is one with the world of deed, as we can see in ancient Hebrew, where the term *dabar* means both "word" and "event." Spoken language, possessing a magical and fluid power, acts as a tool by which the ground of being can be worked. God says, "Let there be light," and there is light; Adam's task is to name the animals, and this creates his dominion over them. Both the world of being and the world of relationship are made by words.

Even silence has meaning: the name of the Hebrew God is secret, not to be spoken, and in many oral cultures the true name of any individual is believed to be identical with that person, and so is concealed for his or her protection. The names of the dead may not be uttered, for fear of drawing their spirits back to this world. To speak a name aloud is to declare oneself willing to summon—the spell, one of the earliest forms of poetry worldwide, is a calling of powers to one's aid by the saying of names. What is spoken is by that speaking made to exist, and what exists is conceived of as that which was once spoken. The earth itself, in many traditions, is a sacred utterance, the singing of the gods.

In MNEMOSYNE's world, in which words hold such singular power and yet come and go in a momentary flash, a quandary arises: how can thought and knowledge be preserved over time? There are only two ways, as Walter Ong has suggested in his book *Orality and Literacy*. One is to transmit an idea by speaking it aloud to someone else, who can then help remember it; this is what we do each time we say to a friend, "Don't let me forget to call Margaret about that." The other strategy is to "think memorable thoughts"—to put thought into a form that will be in itself an aid to memory. The most universal of such forms are the call and response of repetition within variation, and separately or together, meter and rhyme—the two repeating bases for verse—are found at the heart of every literary and oral tradition worldwide. We need only watch an infant learning to speak to see the innate satisfaction that repetition brings. Like dance, lyric and song come into being as original joys that confirm the body's own rhythmic life.

Repetition lies also at the heart of other linguistic devices we associate with poetry's beauty and sensual pleasure. The parallel structures and balanced sentence patterns seen especially in classical Chinese poetry; the alliteration found in the earliest English-language poems; assonance; the thought-patterns of the sonnet or the word-patterns of such rhetorical figures as chiasmus; lists, especially those using anaphora, in which each part begins with the same word—all serve to lead the mind with accuracy from one word to the next. They do this by helping to shape where a thought is going by the recall of where it has been. Consider the literal meaning of this synonym for the act of memory: "recall," to voice again. Repetition embracing variation is the thread of the cloth Mnemosyne wears.

The linguist Roman Jacobson did extensive work on Russian folk proverbs, exploring the ways condensation and the devices of patterned syntax and sound help them survive. In one essay, "Subliminal Verbal Patterning," he shows that highly sophisticated poetic figures and language patterns appear fully formed in the sayings and tales of illiterate peasants. He points out that even thoroughly literate users of memorable patterns do not always do so out of conscious intention— William Blake, for example, stated that complex verbal designs appeared in his work "without Premeditation and even against my Will." The essence of aphorisms and proverbs is to be both linguistically shapely and the briefest possible containers of their own meaning. "A penny saved is a penny earned" and "A stitch in time saves nine" are models not only of compression of content, but also of memorability in their patterns of syntax or sound—the first by repeating its grammatical form and rhythm, the second through half-rhyme and its interwoven *s*s, *t*s, and *i*s. If one remembers such sayings at all, one will remember them not in approximation, but exactly. Unlike ordinary sentences subjected to the forces every child has seen at work in the game of "telephone," these will resist distortion and entropy as they pass from ear to ear.

For those who have been shaped by literacy, proverbs and especially mnemonics offer some sense of the way purely oral memory works. Trying to remember something, we search our minds not for the information itself but for the formulaic saying that holds it in place: "Thirty days hath September," we start to recite, or we hum the tune in which the alphabet is held. Yet these sayings work only for remembrance of the smallest units of meaning. Larger constellations of meaning need something more to survive over time, which has been clarified only in the past half-century by the attempt to understand how the Homeric poems were produced and maintained. What that research has made visible is this: if the threads of memory are spun of the sounds and structures of individual lines, physical embodiment and narrative are the loom on which the epic's astonishing garment is woven.

The seminal theory was worked out in the early 1920s by Milman Parry for a master's thesis at the University of California, Berkeley. Examining the *Iliad* and *Odyssey* Parry realized that the choice of words and phrases at any given point are driven by what he called "the requirements of the shape of the hexameter line." From this insight, he concluded that the Greek poems, though they have come down to us through later transcription, were not originally written at all. Instead, he found in them the marks of a process of oral composition by *rhapsodes*—tellers of tales, or, literally, "stitchers."

Parry and a protégé, Albert B. Lord, tested out this theory in the 1930s by traveling to Serbian villages; Lord's *The Singer of Tales* holds a full account of their work. They found that lengthy narrative poems were still being sung by illiterate singers, to the accompaniment not of a lyre, but of another stringed instrument, the *gusle*. Though no historical situation can precisely duplicate another, what they saw and heard corroborated their hypothesis that the Homeric poems, for all their vastness, were orally composed and handed down. Not only were the twentieth-century bards, called *guslari*, unlettered, but our own age's conceptions both of original authorship and of verbatim memory were, if anything, antithetical to the way they accomplished their task. Rather than memorizing by rote, the guslari drew their songs from a storehouse of formulaic metrical phrases they had learned by listening to other singers since earliest childhood; these formulae were then woven into a web of similarly traditional narrative themes. The idea of individual words is itself a construct of written language—compare the English two-word *Good day* with the French *Bonjour*. One might say, then, that the formulae *are* the words of oral poetry: words that, taken together, form a specialized kind of language created to fulfill the needs of memorability.

A master guslar would perform his own version of a new tale, however lengthy, after only a single hearing, but he first required a pause of at least a night and a day, and preferably a week, in which the piece could "ferment"—precisely the opposite of the way that word-by-word memorization works. And though the guslari boasted they could recite a poem "exactly the same" as they had twenty years earlier, in fact Lord's tape recordings proved that each telling was unique. A rhapsode's real skill, according to Lord, consisted of his ability to weave the story at hand into a new whole appropriate for each audience and occasion of its telling.

If the songs had been found to be repeated verbatim, differences between rhapsodes would be more akin to the differences between actors than between "authors"—and in fact the truest description may lie somewhere between, for the rhapsode does not so much create his tale as offer himself up to become it. One might think also of literal stitchers, quilt-makers, in this context. Though they work with traditional patterns and materials available to all, it is the specific aesthetic choices and abilities of a relative few that mark them as artists. And, like quilt-makers, the rhapsodes are artists almost incidentally: their task is to make something useful for their community, the story that helps to hold it together over time.

Poetry was theater, library, university, on-line service in Mnemosyne's world—its role was nothing less than the preservation and transmission of human knowledge and culture. In *Preface to Plato*, Eric A. Havelock describes how the Homeric poems served as the encyclopedias of the Greek world. Geography, genealogies, laws;

descriptions of how a ship is launched or brought into harbor; accounts of how to behave at a banquet, how not to behave toward the daughter of a priest—all were preserved across both time and distance in the epic's hexameter lines. They were passed on and renewed through public gatherings in which the intermingled, powerful rhythms of voice, lyre, and body were absorbed physically as well as mentally by the listeners. Whether listener or reciter, each participant entered fully into a common dream of what it meant to be Greek and human—a dream larger than any individual mind, that had been put into the care of the Muse. Verse spun a thread of continuity and identity a person could follow through the chaos of a largely unknown and unknowable world.

SOUND-BASED mnemonics, supported by the rhythms of the lyre, hold details accurately in place at the level of the line. Remembrance of larger structures in the epic takes place not in mouth and breath, but within the imaginative mind. This is accomplished perhaps most powerfully by engaging the unfolding powers of plot. As we see in young children, the mind's first way of understanding the world is by story: rehearsing familiar tales, a child constructs a familiar self, as well as a sense of existence as rhythmic, progressive, and meaningfully structured. Narrative both lends itself to repeated tellings and is in itself memorable—listening to an interesting story, we project ourselves vividly into its characters, their experience becoming a part of our own. Narrative, then, uses the structure of time to defeat the ephemerality of time, and, as Havelock has pointed out, a story's episodes can also serve the oral mind as table of contents and index.

The mind of oral memory dwells always in a physical body. Neither emotion nor ideas have yet been abstracted; they live instead in the form of gods and goddesses whose angers, desires, moralities, and jealousies affect human behavior in the form of furious storms, biting gadflies, and irresistibly beautiful singing. Such physical descriptions let us enter a story vividly, as if from within. We do not only receive a powerfully described world in our minds, we occupy it—sleeping in the cradle of its rocky harbors, eating of its honey cakes sprinkled with dark seeds of poppy.

In a culture that likes to think it is founded on the powers of logical, rational mind, the term "imaginary" has taken on overtones of the trivial or the frivolous. Yet the imagination was oral mind's earliest tool for conceiving of the abstract at all, by binding ideas into physical, visual form. Grief at the very existence of death becomes the image of Achilles' two immortal horses lowering their dusty heads to weep over the body of Patroclus. The concept of life's ceaseless abundance, difficult as well as joyous, is carved by Homer and the craftsman-god Hephaestus onto Achilles' shield of war: A bridal procession unfolds near a marketplace argument over the blood-price of a murdered man; ploughmen drink flagons of wine as they pause in their labors; lions tear into the slaughtered body of an ox, oblivious of the nearby baying of dogs; acrobats and courting couples flank the blood-drenched figure of Death, busy harvesting her pick of young men from amid a battle. And all is ultimately enclosed by the great river that bounds the edge of the shield—water circling the realm of what can be seen and heard and touched, beyond which oral consciousness could not go.

These life-holding devices of Mnemosyne, story and physical embodiment, can still be found in the familiar precept given new writers: "Show, don't tell." Now, as twenty-eight hundred years ago, a poet's task is to cast a convincing spell, to create in the mind of another a lasting and particular vision of human experience, whether as sweeping as Homer's or as tightly focused as a single fragment by Sappho. A poem's task is to seduce—its readers or listeners must find in it something irresistible, something to which they want to surrender. The power of beautiful sound and structured language is one such lure; the power of vivid imagining is another; and a third is the human curiosity called forth by story, which lingers not only in poems that are obvious narratives but also in the way good poems root themselves in specificity of situation and event. In any good lyric poem—even one as brief as a haiku—a tiny narrative exists: there is a moment of transformation. Something happens, to writer, to reader, over its course.

This, then, is the world of Mnemosyne, in which all knowledge has been hard won, braced against the erasures of time by generations of singers and their words. In creation stories and early songs and poems worldwide, the strategies of oral mind are the same. It is a mind in which knowledge is embedded in the recital of outward description and actions, and in which new information immediately becomes the basis for a new story. It is a mind in which the complex grammar of subordinate clauses and their finely honed logic has not yet appeared, but, to use Elizabeth Bishop's phrase, "everything [is] only connected by 'and' and 'and.'" Lastly, it is a mind carried through time by the artful weaving of sound. Then, writing arrives—and the possibilities of mind, thought, memory, and poetry are suddenly and irrevocably altered. Much will be retained of Mnemosyne's ways, particularly in the making of poems, but much will also be added to them. And at this moment, we come to another point of poetry's beginning and another Greek god: Hermes, complex and fitting symbol of what is to come.

▾　▾　▾　▾　▾

GUARDIAN of the crossroads and of communication, and inventor of poetry's tools—first the lyre and then the alphabet—Hermes is the patron god of writing. Born long after Mnemosyne, into a world already filled with beings, gods, and stories, he is the last of the gods to join the Greek pantheon and does so out of his own deliberate ambition. Mnemosyne's story is simple: she enters the world, brings her gift of remembrance, and gives birth to her daughters; that is all. The story of Hermes, like his character, is filled with complication and multiplicity. In the paradox that so often holds Greek truth, the messenger god is a trickster. He lies, he jokes, he speaks by indirection as often as he speaks clearly. Tricksters spill with the energy of creation, and true to the form, Hermes loves sex: when the other gods retreat in horror at the sight of Aphrodite trapped aloft in a net with her lover Ares, Hermes only desires her more. Like language, like unsocialized sexuality, he can travel between realms freely—what he wants, he goes after. And it is in his playfulness, irreverence, and disdain for the rules that his capacities for seeing things new, for invention, also reside. He is in many ways the opposite of Mnemosyne, whose power, though it rises in a springlike freshening, is primarily in the service of conservation and continuance. The power of Hermes is that of change.

As a precocious day-old infant, Hermes captures a tortoise outside the cave where he was born. He kills it and, with the immediate and instinctive curiosity of child-mind, guts it. He then proceeds to steal his brother Apollo's herd of fifty sacred oxen, killing two cows as a sacrifice to the gods; seeing some possibility in the material at hand, he uses the intestines of one to make strings for the tortoise's shell—and so fashions the first lyre. When the furious Apollo tracks him down, Hermes calms him by singing a song of praise to his brother; literally enchanted, Apollo agrees to trade the remaining cows for the lyre itself, and in this way becomes the patron god of poetry. Next, Hermes invents the first shepherd's pipe, which he again gives away, this time in exchange for the gift of augury, of "reading" the future. Called before his father, Zeus, he is cautioned to behave more maturely in the future. Zeus then assigns him his duties as a member of the pantheon: the job of messenger and also the care of treaties, commerce, and travelers. This initial meeting of Zeus and Hermes is an interesting moment; in it we can see how the powers of the existing order attempt to acknowledge and include but also contain the new god, force of liberating and chaotic change.

Having created the instruments of music and gained the art of divination—of reading the signs of the world—and with his new responsibilities in mind, Hermes next joins with the Fates in devising a number of new technologies: the alphabet, astronomy (another tool for augury and predicting the future), musical scales, boxing, a system of weights and measures, the cultivation of olives. As master of oaths, Hermes is the god of rhetoric and magical formulae. There is also a rather phallic tale about his invention of fire-making, a technology Prometheus will later steal for humans along with *grammata* (written letters). Throughout Hermes' stories runs the thread of energetic invention—his works are not only artistic but also artful: crafty, clever, and ingenious. What better patron for writing can we imagine than this god whose hallmarks are not only creativity and playfulness, but also the capacity for anarchistic duplicity and lies?

Many themes in the story of Hermes appear as well in that of the Chinese god credited with the invention of writing, Fu Hsi. Creator of musical instruments, Fu Hsi also taught human beings how to domesticate animals and catch fish in nets, devised a system of writing by tying knots in strings, and invented the trigrams used in Chinese divination. Both gods are resourceful producers, holding sway in the realms of art and commerce, and both are strongly connected to the idea of augury as well. Further, the earliest writing known in China appears on the oracle bones of the Shang dynasty (1766-1122 BCE)—generally either the shoulder bones of oxen or the shells of tortoise. Surely the convergence between these two cultures' versions of the origins of writing cannot be entirely an accident. An overlap in the inventions and domains of expertise of the two gods makes a kind of intuitive sense, but why these particular animals reappear (once in myth, once historically) is more of a mystery. For the tortoise, an explanation may come from the markings on the shell, already so much like written signs. The oxen remain more puzzling—except that, as early givers of meat and milk and labor, they are powerful symbols of that moment in which the wild earth's gifts to humankind were domesticated and put to use. In any case, it is in the shape of their powerful heads that the Western alphabet begins—turn the letter *A* on its side and you can still see the vestige of its early Greek form, modeled on the head of an ox with its two protruding horns.

WITH Hermes and the advent of writing a sea-change comes to our relationship to words, to time, and ultimately, to thought. The flowing, present-moment stream of Mnemosyne's unselfconscious recital gives way to the ingenuity of the Trickster, and the mark of Hermes permeates this new way of being in the world. Though writing and reading come late to the world, of the pair the mind of reading arrives first, even in Hermes' own story. Part of its flavor has always been an association with both prediction and the solving of puzzles. Before consciousness learned to transcribe experience into written signs, it read the weather, the herds of wild animals, the first turning leaf, the words and the hearts of others. To read with accuracy the outer world is the most basic work of understanding, the initial action we must bring to the enigmatic data of raw existence. And the results of reading matter: hunters read scat, sailors read the sky, and lovers read one another's every gesture, word, and glance with an intensity of attention they may bring to little else in their lives.

The word *read* comes from Old English and Germanic words having to do with advice-giving, interpretation, and guessing. Further back there is the Latin *ratus,* past participle of the verb *reri,* meaning to count, calculate, or reckon. One cognate is the Middle English *redel:* riddle. This etymology, as well as the myth of Hermes, links the reader of written letters to the early astrologer scanning the star-sprayed darkness, or the priest peering into a slaughtered bird's entrails, interpreting signs. The reader, along with the interpreter of oracles, searches in what is read for an answer useful for going forward wisely in life. But symbols—and particularly words, as many Greek myths show—are perverse. In the face of our human desire for under-standing, they pose riddles before which our ability to read the face of things must either deepen or fail—and how it fails is instructive.

In one myth, which surely dates from the literate age, King Midas inquires of the oracle at Delphi what will happen if he takes his army into battle. The answer returns: "A great kingdom will be over-thrown." Confidently, Midas advanced against Persia, and the king-dom soon overthrown was his own. If Midas had widened his percep-tion of the statement, had "read" the reply to his question not with the self-serving mind of his desires but for what it might mean on its own terms, he might have seen the danger and been spared. Hubris is the tale of the near miss. If you read carelessly, shallowly, or selfishly, this story says, it is at your peril. To be anything less than absolutely atten-tive is to fail to come up to what the deepest nature of reading requires—not least, inclusion of the Trickster's complex ways.

With the arrival of Hermes and written language, as we have seen, speech moves from the tongue and ear into the sense-realm of the eyes. This shift frees the mind of its first, great work of simple remem-brance, and at the same time makes of language something that can be held still, and so subjected to a new care: to new and deeper levels of reading. Though the devices of Mnemosyne continue to permeate written language, the medium (as Marshall McLuhan memorably, alliteratively put it) is also the message. Writing alters consciousness.

Objectified and able to be held at a distance from the self, the written word makes possible a considered survey of the human mind and its contents: once a thought can be looked at once, it can be looked at twice.

Further, once words have been placed into the form of externally perceptible objects, those objects, like individual building blocks, can be moved about independently from one another and put into new relationships, vertical as well as horizontal. The chain of narrative structure can be broken, and thinking is freed of its bonds to time and event. Knowledge formerly held only within personified action expands to a dense field of ideas and propositions, nouns used abstractly, newly complex logical relationships. Thought itself, along with the means of its recording, becomes reified, an object seemingly equivalent to other "things." In the process, consciousness is both liberated and fragmented.

This new mode of thinking affects everyone born into a literate culture, not only those who can read—the ways of literate mind, like the contents of Pandora's box, affect the whole community once they are released. At the core is this: when not only the world of phenomena but also the world of the mind itself can be read, reflection and analysis emerge. With them comes a new sense of what it means to be human, to be a self who can think in a way outside of events and a culture's consensual understandings. Such an individual will be more private, more separate from others—will be able, in a wholly new way, to be not only a carrier of cultural knowledge but an author.

One caution: it may be that scholars have made more of this idea of the private self's roots in literacy than is quite warranted. Our knowledge of what historical oral mind chose to preserve in verse can come only from the first written texts, and while it is true that the Greek epic poems and works such as *Gilgamesh, Beowulf,* or South African praise poems offer more a portrait of "types" than individual lives, the earliest folk songs of Chinese and Japanese literature and the hieroglyph-transcribed love songs of Egypt's New Kingdom, dating from 1300 BCE, are filled with the sense of personal, common life. A girl asks her lover to join her in a bathing pond while she wears her new dress of sheer Memphis linen; a man wishes he might dry himself with the towels that have touched his beloved's face. These long-vanished lovers scarcely seem emblematic of larger forces—they are wholly themselves. Conversely, highly literate twentieth-century societies have made fierce attempts to immerse the private individual into group mind. For many decades, Communist China, Romania, and the Soviet Union suppressed "personal" writing as socially dangerous; in this country, recurrent attacks on artists as "un-American" show that wariness of individualized expression is hardly confined to Marxist regimes.

What is considered worth remembering becomes what is considered important; even the limited democracy of ancient Athens could not have been conceived in a culture concerned only with accounts of leaders and gods. The personal *is* political. We may wonder whether the concept of self-governance could have arisen without the respect granted Sappho and Archilochus, who each used Mnemosyne's memorable meters to carry the passions of daily life.

A two-thousand-year record of diaries, journals, pillow books, and "confessions" shows the way putting thoughts on paper allows a person to develop a deepened sense of individual life as well as independence of opinion. Private reflection creates the freedom to venture past what is generally held to be true—within the refuge of a journal's bound pages, one can hold an opinion at odds with others and not pay an immediate social price. The Trickster's cultural role is to counter rigidity and the forms of authority, and the tricksterish effects of literacy are ultimately personalizing and democratic, however slowly the process unfolds—which may be one reason that many cultures made writing a carefully restricted skill, kept especially from women. By allowing its practitioners to think, see, and act for themselves, as well as by its ability to safeguard the already known, writing allows originality and idiosyncrasy of perception and statement to emerge.

The same holds true for the effects of literacy on the more formal aspects of poetry—the memorability inherent especially in the printed word, which enables the exact reproduction of visual forms for the first time, allows the development of the concrete poem (poems written in the shape of what they describe, first used in English by the seventeenth-century poet George Herbert in his poem "The Altar," arranged in the shape of a cross), the free verse line, and eventually even more highly individualized arrangements of poems on the page. The typographical play in the poems of E. E. Cummings or the overprintings and strike-outs of Susan Howe are only the most recent of the new branches that Hermes grafts onto poetry's oral roots. Relatively fresh, they still surprise; yet each of Hermes' inventions seemed revolutionary, odd, even threatening, at the time of its first appearance. Plato, who lived at the pivot point of the oral-literate transition in Greece, shows Socrates condemning not only the poets, symbols of the old oral culture, but also the newly common practice of writing, which he asserted would weaken both memory and the ability to search out truth—written words, unlike debators, cannot argue back.

▾　▾　▾　▾　▾

T HE old ways were designed to persist, and the goddess of continuity is powerful. Even this essay uses one of Mnemosyne's strategies for thought, in describing poetry's evolution through the personified figures of two Greek gods. Still, once preserved, thought was freed of the need to be memorable. The work of history, philosophy, theology, moral allegory, and science could be approached in ways outside the rhapsode's devices of meter and sound, and eventually these forms of thinking moved virtually entirely into prose. Quite late, the novel emerges—related to the epic in some ways and yet wholly different.

Over two and a half millennia of literacy, the topics poetry approaches have slowly shifted. Though a poet such as Robert Frost or Maya Angelou may at times be invited to contribute to a public occasion, the work of forging community has gone over to song—to cultural anthems such as "We Shall Overcome" or "Imagine," or to whatever song is chosen to accompany the current political campaign. Even poems contemplating larger cultural issues (Auden's "September 1, 1939," Eliot's "The Wasteland," Pound's "Cantos") do so within a highly individualized frame. A few recent poems attempting to voice directly the experience of a community come to mind—Gwendolyn Brooks's "We Real Cool: The Pool Players" is one example, even its title subtly echoing the old Greek chorus. Still, this outwardly simple poem asks of the reader a far more sophisticated understanding than does preliterate oral work, and the same is true of the writing of recent experimental poets who seek to escape subjectivity in their work.

In the realm of the personal lyric, love poems, religious hymns, and elegies arrived early, but accounts of bearing and raising children have entered the main Western tradition only in the last few decades, along with descriptions of car repair, factory work, and air travel. These additions stem not only from the changed demographics of poets; they are also a sign of our altered conception of the lyric itself. Late twentieth-century writings wrestle with the perennial questions of poetry, but they do so from the point of view of the individual, not the tribe: Hermes' task is not to speak for the whole but to create new depth through disruption, question, introspection, challenge. Poetry has responded in kind. And yet—

One line of *The Homeric Hymn to Hermes* suggests that Hermes was, in fact, destined to be Mnemosyne's chosen consort. If a wedding of Mnemosyne and Hermes is the source of poetry as we now know it, how should we summarize what each partner brings to the nuptial bed? Mnemosyne shows us how to make thought memorable through the story, image, compression, linguistic structure, and sound; Hermes keeps language flexible and energetic, playful, experimental, free to change. Mnemosyne provides the place of beginning, the world of human event, of what is and has been; Hermes' realm is revision, seeing what emerges when the mind is able to look back on itself—how a tortoise, seen freshly, might become a lyre. Mnemosyne gives the forms and strategies of verse a central authority and role that continue to resonate at poetry's core; Hermes forges of these forms a tool to sing of new knowledge, new ways to know.

While Mnemosyne and Hermes bring different dowries to the poetry we now know, each also supports the other's gifts. Mnemosyne's eternal present does in fact accommodate change—like the old goddesses of Europe whose temples were later rededicated to Mary, the Muse is not only capable of changing her story, she will do so whenever the present situation alters its needs. Similarly, Hermes' ingenuity works also in the service of remembrance—both the lyre and written language are technologies that preserve words through time. Poetry's strategies remain a pendulum swinging between the gifts of both these figures, and each shift of aesthetic in poetry over time can be viewed as a negotiation between the desires of Mnemosyne and those of Hermes. By the friction and tensions these two approaches engender, poetry is continually renewed.

The turn to common speech by the English Romantic poets, for example, can be viewed as Hermes breaking loose from an overly codified and constricting poetic tradition. And in just the past few decades of American poetry, we have seen the aesthetic strategy of the deep image and its poetry of physical embodiment challenged by the more hermetic practitioners of language poetry; then, in the 1980s, neoformalists and proponents of the new narrative appeared to champion Mnemosyne's devices in turn, to balance the rise of a highly conceptualized and page-based poetics. Charles Olson's projective verse, based on the rhythms of the natural breath, and Allen Ginsberg's "Kaddish" are recognizably in the lineage of oral poetry; John Ashbery and Jorie Graham work more in the tradition of subtle literate mind. Questions of fragmentation versus wholeness; of whether meaning and coherence are the products of a dominating cultural authority or the natural workings of mind; of infinitely open-ended possible readings or the degree to which an author's intentions matter—all are matters of passionately partisan debate, a literary Trojan War in which these two Olympians each have their chosen heroes. Yet every writer is nourished by the full spectrum, the full history of the tradition. New strategies take their revolutionary meaning from their relationship with the forms that have gone before, and however much memory may shift its devices, it does not ever completely abandon the old: each step of a journey enters and alters the body of the person who makes it.

For the Greek rhapsode, the idea of a poem as a poem may not even have existed—and certainly our conception of a poet did not. The "maker"—what the Greek word for poet literally means—was not the individual self, but the entire culture, re-presenting and remaking itself and the world in song, through the Muse. The golden age of poetry so often mourned was not the age of Eliot or Frost, or of Wordsworth, Keats, Shakespeare, Dante, or even Sappho. It was the age of Mnemosyne, in which poetry was humankind's one account of the whole, and the poet was, in fact, the acknowledged legislator of the race. Yet how much has been gained by that wholeness's breaking into separate letters, into the many parts—not least the ability to hold the idiosyncratic music and knowledge of individual lives. And conversely, however strange each new development may seem, every poem remains an attempt to name with fidelity some complex aspect of the human experience and keep it available through time. We peer into the new poem with the old hope: that we might find there a few words to illumine more widely our passage through the dark woods and brightly lit cities of the fleeting, time-bound world. And the art of poetry remains a daughter of Remembrance—of our wish to feel joined to some fabric that both gives meaning to and is made meaningful by the part of it we are.

Writing and the Threshold Life

▼ ▼ ▼ ▼ ▼ ▼ ▼ ▼ ▼

At the start of the fourteenth-century Nō play *Sotoba Komachi* (Komachi on the Stupa), a priest from Mount Koya travels toward Kyoto, discussing Buddhist teachings with his attendant. The first words they speak are these lines:

In the worn-down mountains are secret places,
in the worn-down mountains are hidden places,
but the true depths, surely, are in the human heart.

The Buddha of the past is long ago vanished,
the Buddha of the future has not yet arrived,
and we, as in a dream, are born into the time between,
not knowing what we should understand as Real.
Only by chance were we born into human form,
only by chance were we lucky enough to hear the teachings of
    Thusness,
to receive the seeds of enlightenment into our hands.

We have only one intention in our hearts,
single as the single layer
of the black cloth robes we wear—
to know the self before birth.
Knowing the self before birth, we would be free—
there would be no parents to tie us to this world,
no children to tie our thoughts to this world.
Though we travel a thousand miles now,
it is not far—these fields where we sleep,
these mountains where we rest, these are our true home.
Now let us pause a while.

An old woman dressed in rags enters the stage from the other side, her white hair wild, her body bent with age. The audience knows it is the ninth-century poet Ono no Komachi—in legend, not only the most accomplished poet but also the most beautiful woman of her time. She probably had at least one child, but she never married. Instead she took many lovers, treating some harshly, being treated harshly by others. When she grew too old to continue serving at court, Komachi retired to a small, thatched hut outside the city walls. There, though her reputation as a poet never faltered, Komachi herself lived on in obscurity, ending her days a half-mad crone wandering the mountain trails. It is this figure—the aged and disarrayed woman who left the capital's life of the center and came to dwell at the periphery in a number of different ways—who carries within her story a wisdom still essential to the writing life.

She speaks:

I am a floating reed,
waiting an invitation from the water.
A floating reed,
but no water asks me to come.

In the past, I held myself high—
bewitching, they said,
my hair graceful as a kingfisher's crest,
my body like willow boughs swaying in a spring breeze.
My voice, like a nightingale's,
opened more lovely than the murmuring
bush-clover blossoms heavy with falling dew.

Now, everyone shuns me,
even the most common women find me loathsome.
In this shame of age,
unhappy days, unhappy months heap up,
and I have become a crone of a hundred years.
I fear the eyes of men now,
fear that someone, seeing, might say "It is she!"
Only at nightfall, by moonlight, do I go out.
Avoiding all eyes,
avoiding the guards of the palace,
I hide among trees that hide also the tombs of lovers,
the mountain of autumn.

Look, in the moonlight, on the river, a barge—
who can the rower be, who can it be?

No.
I am tired, worn.
I will sit on this half-rotted stump and rest.

At this point, the two priests come upon Komachi, and immediately
begin to berate her:

You, old beggar—
can't you see that you sit on a stupa,
a sacred symbol, body of the Buddha?
Get up at once, go sit somewhere else.

Komachi answers submissively at first:

> You say it is a stupa,
> but I do not see any sign —
> no words, no carvings either.
> It just looks like the rotting stump of a tree.

The senior priest replies:

> Just as a decaying log
> deep in the mountains bursts into flower
> and you know it's a tree,
> so it is with this log sculpted into the Buddha's body.
> How could you fail to see?

Komachi:

> But I too am a half-buried tree.
> My heart still opens into flowers . . .
> I might offer them up in this place.
> Still, why do you insist
> that this old stump is the Buddha's body?

They then begin a debate over stupas and their symbolism, and the priest quotes the saying,

> "To look even once on a stupa
> is to become free of the Three Evil Paths."

Komachi, grown bold now, counters him with another saying, taken from the Flower Garland Sutra:

> "One whole-hearted thought
> is enough to attain the mind of Buddha" —
>
> Do you think this a lesser way?

The attendant then says:

If you aspire to the mind of Buddha,
you should despise this world and its ways.

Komachi answers at once his implicit criticism that she has not taken
formal Buddhist vows, as they have:

It is not through outer appearance
that I have renounced the world,
it is in my heart.

The priest replies:

It is because you are heartless
that you failed to recognize
the Buddha's body.

And Komachi responds:

No, it is because it is the Buddha's body
that I chose to approach it!

The attendant:

And still,
without any gratitude,
you sat on it!

Komachi:

It was already lying down, this stupa—
why should it be wrong that I also rest?

The priest:

That goes against Right Action.

Komachi:

But Wrong Action may lead to salvation too!

The priest, the attendant, and Komachi then speak the following
words together, in alternating lines, though within the conventions of
Nō it is clear the thoughts are hers:

> There are stories
> that even a wicked man
> can know the mercy
> of the teachings of Compassion,
> that even a fool
> can become awakened
> through the teachings of Wisdom.
> Evil may become Goodness,
> even the Passions
> can lead to the Mind of the Way.
> The root of enlightenment
> is not some tree
> that can be planted or not,
> the clear mirror of awakening
> has no need of a stand.
> In truth, when all things
> are known as One,
> there is no difference at all
> between Buddhas and sentient beings.
> If to save foolish mortals by any means
> has been the one true vow
> from the beginning,
> then surely even wrong actions
> must lead to Awakened Mind.

At this, the priest and attendant give in:

> You are an outcast beggar
> who is truly enlightened!

And saying this, they touch their heads to the earth three times in
homage.

THAT is the culmination of the first part of the play. Next, the priests ask the woman who she is, and discover to their amazement that they are speaking with the legendary Komachi. They recall her former beauty and glory and comment on her circumstances now: her white eyebrows and hair, the sack she carries around her neck with only a few grains of dried millet and beans for food, her clothing covered with dirt, her tattered straw raincoat, her raveling hat of woven reeds.

Komachi describes the madness that comes over her at times; it is then visibly played out, as Komachi's spirit is taken over by the angry ghost of a former lover. He recalls the nights he waited outside her door in the darkness and wind, through first the time of falling leaves and rain, then of falling snow. Reliving his suffering, Komachi cries out in pain and ultimately, also, in compassion for the lover, who died on the ninety-ninth night of the hundred she asked of him to prove his steadfastness. The play ends with her vow to continue traveling the path of Buddhist enlightenment until both their spirits are freed.

▾   ▾   ▾   ▾   ▾

THERE are many ways to look at this story and its images. It invites our contemplation in its presentation of Buddhist understanding, as a protofeminist story, for the luminosity of its poetry, and for the pathos and dignity of the human tale it holds. Here though, I would like to consider the play in the light of a concept from anthropology—to look at the aged Komachi as a figure who exemplifies the realm of the liminal, a word derived from the Latin *limen*, meaning "threshold."

In *The Ritual Process*, anthropologist Victor Turner describes the liminal as the time and space of transition integral to all rites of passage. Entering this condition, a person leaves behind his or her old identity and dwells in a threshold state of ambiguity, openness, and indeterminacy. Only afterward may the initiate enter into new forms of identity and relationship, rejoining the everyday life of the culture—but now as adult or married person, as healer or holder of clan secrets.

A number of specific characteristics mark this state of being "betwixt and between." First, the initiate undergoes the removal of both identity and status—he or she becomes nameless; conventional clothing is forgone; the usual constraints of gender no longer apply. Ordinarily forbidden behavior is now allowed, or, conversely, the person may enter into an extreme discipline equally foreign to conventional life. Often there is a period of silence and of nondoing, of fasting or going without sleep. Threshold persons are treated as outsiders and exiles, separated from the group, reviled, ignored. Akin in status to the unborn or the dead, they are not present in the community in any normal sense. Possessing nothing, they descend into invisibility and darkness, and—symbolically or literally—abandon both the physical and the ideological structures of society for a wilderness existence.

More is changed during this threshold period than simply the understanding of self: free of all usual roles, a person experiences community differently as well. The liminal is not opposite to, but the necessary companion of, identity and particularity—a person who steps outside her usual position falls away from any singular relationship to others and into oneness with the community as a whole. Within the separateness of liminality, connectedness itself is remade. A line of Gary Snyder's describes the dynamic this way: "Awareness of emptiness brings forth the heart of compassion."

Entire societies, as well as individuals, at times enter the condition of threshold for renewal. During the Middle Ages, much of Europe celebrated a holiday of the liminal, the Feast of Fools. A mock king or bishop was elected (often the village idiot); anyone of the slightest power was subjected to ridicule and parody by everyone else; and general chaos and celebration were the order of a day in which nothing was exempt from reversal.

Halloween is one remnant of such a ritual, a night when all members of the community agree to open their doors to intimacy with ghosts and demons, with vandalism and trickery. It is to just such an opening that Czeslaw Milosz alludes in his poem "Ars Poetica?" Describing the writer as a person who must be willing to be inhabited by a "daimonion," the poet asks, "What reasonable man would like to be a city of demons?" Yet despite the genuine danger of such a course, it is exactly this permeability that poetry asks:

> The purpose of poetry is to remind us
> how difficult it is to remain just one person,
> for our house is open, there are no keys in the doors,
> and invisible guests come in and out at will.
>
> *(trans. Czeslaw Milosz and Lillian Vallee)*

Milosz's words are themselves a key: they tell us why entrance into the liminal is fundamental to the life of writing. Speaking from the point of view of multiplicity, betweenness, and visitation, the writer can become a person in whom both individuality and community may ripen into true expression. In the work of such a person, what lies beyond the conventional, simplified, and "authorized" versions of a culture's narratives can find voice. A newly broadened conception of being is made available to all.

FROM the Nō play's opening words, Komachi's story places us deep in the realm of threshold: amid worn-down mountains and hiddenness and the uncertain world that exists between past and future buddhas. But while the two priests are liminal figures themselves—as all monks are—they also represent the world of fixed identity and structure, of society's habitual ways of thinking. The priests' understanding of Buddhist teaching isn't wholly incorrect, but it is incomplete. Their role in the play is to be instructed and initiated by Komachi, whose long immersion in hardship and stripped-down being has freed her from conventional ideas and brought her to a wisdom more keenly honed.

The distinctions are sometimes subtle, but present. The monks say that the fields they find themselves in are their one true home, but for Komachi this is not doctrine, it is literal truth. And though as *unsui*, "wandering clouds," the priests have taken vows to become home-leavers, they are in fact passers-through, traveling from their home temple on Mount Koya to the capital. Komachi lives permanently outside society's structures—forgotten, separated from her former identity, her roof falling open to the winds and moon. One of her best-known poems describes both her dwelling and her life:

> This abandoned house,
> shining,
> in a mountain village.
> How many nights
> has the autumn moon spent here?

Komachi situates herself from the start in the nonhuman, calling herself a floating reed. Even while remembering her time at court, each physical comparison she makes draws from nature: willow branches, kingfishers, nightingales. In age, though, she has truly entered exile and anonymity, living without name beyond the walls of the city, venturing out only at night. She dresses in clothes barely distinguished from the wild grasses and reeds they were made from; she lives by begging; she who was once beautiful is now loathed and reviled by even the lowest members of society. Each of these qualities marks Komachi as a liminal person. Her advanced years, as well, place her on the cusp between life and death.

And what of that other work of liminality, the way threshold existence opens into a more capacious sense of community? In the debate over the stupa, Komachi sits squarely on the side of nonseparation and oneness: a fallen log and the body of the Buddha are to her the same. And just as this symbolic stupa has substantially rotted back into the earth, so has she, the once-great poet who calls herself "also a half-buried tree." Her chosen path to awakening lies not in wearing the formal black robes of a monk, but in cultivating the single-minded intention to attain the Buddha's Way. She seeks this without fanfare, amid the common life of this world, and when the two monks speak of trying to break free of the attachments that come of human birth, she speaks for a different path—the belief that even wrong actions and a life of passion may bring a wholehearted person into awakening. Remember, too, that the speech holding these ideas is spoken in unison, the joined voices of Nō chant setting their seal upon connected, embodied life.

Komachi's chosen path is immersion rather than escape, oneness rather than separation, and above all a radical allegiance to the nondual. As the play unfolds, she is shown as possessed: so permeable of identity that another spirit may enter hers as a road toward both their salvation. This too is the way of the threshold person, who, like the Buddhist bodhisattva who vows not to enter enlightenment until every last blade of grass may enter as well, is engaged in her work on behalf of everyone, not only for the individual self.

Komachi's wisdom comes from her entrance into the liminal wilderness beyond the capital, but also from her earlier willingness to experience the life of relationship and the causes and effects of her own karma—from the bewildering mountain paths of the human heart. Komachi's way is to live through every part of her life. And when the priests recognize her understanding, they no longer speak in terms of doctrine, but touch their foreheads to the moist earth in acknowledgment of her deeper truth.

▾　　▾　　▾　　▾　　▾

IMMERSION in the life of the world; the willingness to be inhabited by and speak for others, including those beyond the realm of the human—these are the practices not just of the bodhisattva, but of the writer. *Sotoba Komachi* offers the story of a poet, and so carries particular interest for those who write. It shows how the life of the threshold can lead to both permeability and knowledge, offering, in Dōgen's phrase, a way to study the self, forget the self, and awaken into the ten thousand things.

For most members of a community, the liminal is a point of transition, entered briefly, at a particular time, in passage toward something else; such persons are dipped into nonidentity and self-forgetfulness in order to change who they are. For some, though, the liminal becomes their only dwelling-place—becomes home. A writer must invent for himself how to live in this way. But another example of the long-standing threshold person, as we have seen, is the monk, the wanderer-among-clouds, and to consider the life of monastics may prove useful in better understanding the writer's task and role.

A monk's needs for clothing, food, and refuge (in symbol, if not always in actuality) are traditionally satisfied at society's margins, using what those at the center consider extraneous or worthless. St. Francis of Assisi abandoned the silk of his wealthy upbringing for a habit of rough brown cloth; the *okesa*, or Buddhist priest's robe, is a patchwork garment, originally sewn of redyed rags that would otherwise have been thrown away—cloth singed by fire, gnawed by oxen or mice, or worn by the dead. The monk dresses, then, in the discarded, abandoned, and unneeded. Similarly, a monk eats solely what has been donated to the community or placed in the begging bowl; one of Teresa of Avila's greatest difficulties lay in persuading both Church and civil authorities to allow her Reformed Carmelite nuns to live by precarious charity rather than under the protection of an endowment. The monk embraces the margin geographically as well: the original followers of the Buddha retired to the peripheral life of the forests during the rainy season, not to the city, and early Christian monks made their place of practice the desert. Even present-day Buddhist and Catholic monastic communities are usually found in the country, or, if in the cities, in the worst parts—the Tenderloins, the ghettos.

Monks are recyclers, composters—out of waste and communal labor they create subsistence, beauty, and wealth. This is the work of the threshold: to step into places of seeming barrenness, emptiness, or neglect and bring back an abundance new-coined. For writers, as for monks, to take on this work often means leaving the mainstream in outward ways, abandoning the world of ordinary jobs and housing; the garret life is found up literal stairs as well as within the steep reaches of the psyche. In its deepest sense, though, threshold life for a writer has to do with a changed relationship to language and culture itself. In writing lit by a liminal consciousness, the most common words take on the sheen of treasure—transformed in meaning for the entire community because they have been dipped in the mind of openness and connection.

THE THRESHOLD brings its riches, but its barrenness contributes as well. The nonwriting writer, the monk who cannot pray, and the homeless street person all have a role; a healthy society grants them that role in a way that does not deny their essential grace. The Bible describes a right relationship between society's center and margin this way: "When thou cuttest down thine harvest in thy field, and hast forgot a sheaf, thou shalt not go again to fetch it: it shall be for the stranger, for the fatherless, and for the widow: that the Lord thy God may bless thee in all the work of thine hands" (Deuteronomy 24:19).

As novelist Marilynne Robinson has written, it matters that not only orphans and widows are permitted this gleaning, but also the true outsider: the passing stranger. And it matters, too, that the ones who are granted the trees' last olives, the late-ripening grapes, forgotten wheat, and coat pocket's loose quarters, are dignified by their position. Through them, the Bible says, the community is blessed—an exchange still held in the "bless you" street people sometimes murmur when accepting a gift. The same wisdom might be remembered in the debates over whether there should be public funding of the arts, or whether we are willing to share our places of habitation with the coyote, the cougar, the wolf, and the fringe-toed lizard. Generosity to the stranger acknowledges that community exists beyond one's own family, social group, species. It requires an altruism beyond any possibility of repayment, even to the point of surrendering what we might rather keep: an extra three sheep on an overgrazed commons; an overly fixed idea of what is beautiful or of the rightness of the current social order.

"Awareness of emptiness brings forth the heart of compassion." As Lewis Hyde pointed out in *The Gift*, it is in the spirit of nonpossession and surrender that art flourishes best. This aspect of threshold makes the liminal writer not only an independent thinker but an engaged one—when a person identifies with the full range of citizens of a place, sentient and nonsentient, he or she cannot help but speak on their behalf.

▾   ▾   ▾   ▾   ▾

THE CHINESE Zen teacher Lin-chi (Rinzai) described enlightenment as becoming a "person of no rank": the person who knows his true nature, like the ordinary person when in the liminal state of transition, is free of the forms of status. To be of "no rank" is to be equal with everyone, whether beggar or king. A parish priest confesses both local prince and village fool; Saint Francis wrote of

Brother Wind and Sister Water, and treated all creation as the radiant image of God. Writers, too, must be persons of no rank, for whom no part of existence is less—or more—holy than the rest. The writer turns to the inconsequential and almost invisible weeds for meaning as much as to the glorious blossoms, values the dark parts of the story as much as its light. Milton is in love with Lucifer. Shakespeare's affections go with Caliban at least as much as with Ariel, Thomas Hardy's with the fallen Tess. Galway Kinnell has said, "The secret title of every good poem might be 'Tenderness'"; these words too are free of rank—for the writer to write at all, he or she must cultivate a heart that opens in tenderness to all things.

A few years ago, I wrote a poem that looks at this question:

Late Prayer

Tenderness does not choose its own uses.
It goes out to everything equally,
circling rabbit and hawk.
Look: in the iron bucket,
a single nail, a single ruby—
all the heavens and hells.
They rattle in the heart and make one sound.

The poem is called a prayer because in writing it I was asking, during a time of difficulty, for such a mind and heart; but I hope it is useful in general as well. A writer cannot identify only with the rabbit, or with the hawk—standing squarely in the threshold, one must include both. A ruby is no more valuable than a nail; the sound of one in a shaken metal bucket is no different from the other. Both will be needed, if we want to include the world in our words.

A well-known Zen saying is Seng-ts'an's, "The perfect way is not difficult, only avoid picking and choosing." In human life we will always do one thing and not another, but Seng-ts'an knew that such choices can still be made within a fundamental nonattachment. If you side too much with the rabbit, the hawks will starve. If you side too much with the hawk, there will be no more rabbits. It is up to the writer to recognize everything that happens to her as gift, to love each thing that comes under the eye's contemplation, inner or outer. To set up straw men is not only a failure of heart—it will also be an inevitable failure of writing. In this, the lessons of ecology, Zen, and artistic craft are the same.

To abandon rank may also mean abandoning name; as in Komachi's story, anonymity is one mark of the liminal. When a gap opens between the old and the new during a rite of passage, the self enters into an undivided life—both who we are and who we might become vanishes. It is just then, when all is permeable, unparticularized, unborn, that a new way of being may emerge.

See how it is described in the opening stanza of Pablo Neruda's "Poetry":

> And it was at that age ... Poetry arrived
> in search of me. I don't know, I don't know where
> it came from, from winter or a river.
> I don't know how or when,
> no, they were not voices, they were not
> words, nor silence,
> but from a street I was summoned,
> from the branches of night,
> abruptly from the others,
> among violent fires
> or returning alone,
> there I was without a face
> and it touched me.

> *(trans. Alastair Reid)*

"Show me your face before your parents were born," says the Buddhist koan alluded to by the priests in *Sotoba Komachi*. For Neruda, that face becomes a poetry of all things: a long praise-song to salt in the mines and in the ocean, to a wristwatch ticking in the night's darkness like a tiny saw cutting time, to the dead body of a fish in the market. In the light of the poet's abundance of heart and imagination, we remember the threshold is a place at once empty and full. It is on the margins, where one thing meets another, and in the times of transition, that ecosystems are most rich and diverse—birds sing, and deer, fish, and mosquitoes emerge to feed at dawn and at dusk.

The gate to this richness, for Neruda, lay in that first moment when he surrendered his narrow identity to be touched by a life larger than his own. Wang Wei, writing during China's T'ang dynasty, described it as well: "In a former life I was a poet—a mistake—and my old body used to belong to a painter. . . . My name and public face may speak of who I once was, but of this my heart knows nothing." Han-shan, another poet of classical China, put it as a question: "Who can leap the world's ties and sit with me among the white clouds?" A similar surrender of self appears in Emily Dickinson: "I'm nobody," she wrote in 1861, and meant it, this woman who habitually likened herself to the most common of flowers, a daisy.

BOTH Dickinson and Walt Whitman are examples of American writers who stepped fully, if by different means, into the life of threshold. Dickinson retired from the public world, changed her clothing to white in a private ritual of status-leaving, and ordained herself into the wholehearted practice of the word. Her attic writing room in Amherst recalls the woven-branch shelter into which the ceremonial initiate retires. Whitman's version of the role was closer to the chameleon liminality of the Trickster; in his passionate espousal of democracy and all its citizens, he freed himself from society's structures and seemliness, and became a person who has studied the self, forgotten the self, and awakened, in poem after poem, into the ten thousand things:

> Space and Time! now I see it is true, what I guess'd at,
> What I guess'd when I loaf'd on the grass,
> What I guess'd while I lay alone in my bed,
> And again as I walk'd the beach under the paling stars of the
>   morning.

Threshold rings clear through these lines, the poet engaged first in nondoing, then out walking during the transition from night to day. The poem continues,

> My ties and ballasts leave me, my elbows rest in sea-gaps,
> I skirt sierras, my palms cover continents,
> I am afoot with my vision.
>
> By the city's quadrangular houses—in log huts, camping with
>   lumbermen,
> Along the ruts of the turnpike, along the dry gulch and rivulet bed,
> Weeding my onion-patch or hoeing rows of carrots and parsnips,
>   crossing savannas, trailing in forests,
> Prospecting, gold-digging, girdling the trees of a new purchase,
> Scorch'd ankle-deep by the hot sand, hauling my boat down the
>   shallow river,
> Where the panther walks to and fro on a limb overhead, where the
>   buck turns furiously at the hunter,
> Where the rattlesnake suns his flabby length on a rock, where the
>   otter is feeding on fish,
> Where the alligator in his tough pimples sleeps by the bayou,
> Where the black bear is searching for roots or honey, where the
>   beaver pats the mud with his paddle-shaped tail;

Over the growing sugar, over the yellow-flower'd cotton plant, over
the rice in its low moist field,

Over the sharp-peak'd farm house, with its scallop'd scum and
slender shoots from the gutters,

Over the western persimmon, over the long-leav'd corn, over the
delicate blue-flower flax,

Over the white and brown buckwheat, a hummer and buzzer there
with the rest,

Over the dusky green of the rye as it ripples and shades in the
breeze . . .

This sentence rolls on, naming the self as everything and every-
where, "a hummer and buzzer there with the rest," for another sixty-
seven lines before it is done.

No poet in the English-language tradition speaks more explicitly
from the threshold than Whitman, particularly in the way he links the
marginal to the community of the whole. The *communitas,* as Turner
calls it, is not about the disappearance of the one into the many, but
about the recognition of each particular one as an equal part of the
many, none to be called better or worse, none to be hidden, none to be
excluded. "I will not make poems with reference to parts, / But I will
make poems, songs, thoughts, with reference to ensemble," Whitman
declares, and enacts this vow everywhere.

In that capacious life-work, *Leaves of Grass,* he says:

I am of old and young, of the foolish as much as the wise,
Regardless of others, ever regardful of others,
Maternal as well as paternal, a child as well as a man,
Stuffed with the stuff that is coarse, and stuffed with the stuff
that is fine.

and a little later:

These are the thoughts of all men in all ages and all lands, they
      are not original with me,
If they are not yours as much as mine they are nothing or next
      to nothing,
If they do not enclose everything they are next to nothing . . .

Throughout his work, Whitman takes his stand with the unwanted
and the outcast. He speaks for them, embraces them, and ultimately,
as in these lines from "Song of Myself," becomes them:

For me the keepers of convicts shoulder their carbines and keep
      watch,
It is I let out in the morning and barr'd at night.

Not a mutineer walks handcuff'd to jail but I am
      handcuff'd to him and walk by his side,
(I am less the jolly one there, and more the silent one with sweat on
      my twitching lips.)

Not a youngster is taken for larceny but I go up too, and am tried
      and sentenced.

Not a cholera patient lies at the last gasp but I also lie at the last gasp,
My face is ash-color'd, my sinews gnarl, away from me people retreat.

Askers embody themselves in me and I am embodied in them,
I project my hat, sit shame-faced, and beg.

There are lines, too, in which Whitman openly rejects ordinary
society for threshold existence, where live both mystery and joy. There
is the famous, "I think I could turn and live with animals," and there is
this:

When I Heard the Learned Astronomer

When I heard the learn'd astronomer,
When the proofs, the figures, were ranged in columns before me,

When I was shown the charts and diagrams, to add, divide, and
    measure them,
When I sitting heard the astronomer where he lectured with much
    applause in the lecture room,
How soon unaccountable I became tired and sick,
Till rising and gliding out I wander'd off by myself,
In the mystical moist night-air, and from time to time,
Look'd up in perfect silence at the stars.

My point—if one can make a point amid Whitman's abundance—
is that only by choosing to live as a person of the threshold could
Whitman throw off the limits of what he was "permitted" to say, the
limits of what he was "permitted" to be, and speak finally for and as a
cosmos.

Dickinson's threshold path, of necessity, was different—more
inward, traveled almost completely within the grounds of her family
home and in the privacy carved of her own heart's language. But she,
like Whitman, made her way to a stance of "betwixt and between,"
intermingling the awareness of larger society and a solitude that per-
mits embracing. In one letter to Thomas Wentworth Higginson she
wrote:

> Of "shunning Men and Women"—they talk of Hallowed things,
> aloud—and embarrass my Dog—He and I dont object to them, if
> they'll exist their side. I think Carlo would please you—He is dumb,
> and brave—I think you would like the Chestnut Tree, I met in my
> walk. It hit my notice suddenly—and I thought the Skies were in
> Blossom—
>   Then there's a noiseless noise in the Orchard—that I let persons
> hear—

In this passage Dickinson moves away from the more obvious
kinds of social connection, but toward another: intimacy with her dog

Carlo, with the chestnut tree she "meets" in its almost overpowering beauty, and with that "noiseless noise" in the orchard that she alone, perhaps, may midwife into the attention of "persons." In this last gesture, the work of making communitas clearly appears. Dickinson did not forget society—her characteristic gesture is a simultaneous retreat and advance. She knew that withdrawal itself was her best path to essential experience, and even to simple communication, and so she placed herself unwaveringly in a liminal intimacy: letters preferred to meetings, visitors to the house met only by her presence just beyond the parlor door.

Yet Dickinson's work, like Whitman's, stands finally free of societal expectations. There is the poem in which this writer, who knew her own worth and who composed close to two thousand poems over her life, states that "Publication—is the Auction / Of the Mind of Man"—and the auction she would have had in mind, as Galway Kinnell has pointed out, was the auction of slaves. There is also a letter to Higginson in which she wrote unabashedly, with her characteristic leaping juxtaposition, "You kindly ask for my Blossoms and Books—I have read but a little recently—Existence has overpowered Books. Today, I slew a Mushroom—" For any writer who has ever felt woefully underdiligent as a reader, there is consolation here.

Open Dickinson's poems almost anywhere and you find her declaring her liminal status:

Between my Country—and the Others—
There is a Sea—

And yet, as Komachi offered her heart-flowers of a half-buried tree, so Dickinson does as well, in this poem's concluding lines:

But Flowers—negotiate between us—
As Ministry.

Where Whitman proclaimed himself male and female, embracing sex and the body, Dickinson seemingly (though perhaps not entirely: there remains the mystery of the "Dear Master" letters, and the intense passion of certain poems) turned away from sex, certainly away from the conventional female life-course of her time, and so freed herself as well of some of gender's hold on her identity. In one letter to Louise and Frances Norcross, she signed herself, intriguingly, "Brother Emily." Both poets rejected organized religion, yet both were ecstatics: the holy infuses everything around them. Each belongs to the lineage of the mystics, and to the tradition of inclusive paradox frequently found in female wisdom figures—in Komachi, with her praise of Wrong Action as a path to enlightenment; in the speaker of the Gnostic Gospel "The Thunder: Perfect Mind," who calls herself wife and virgin, holy one and whore, force of joining and of dissolving; in the female figure of Wisdom who appears in Proverbs: 8, present in the world from its birth.

Another aspect of mystical paradox is the willing embrace of pain—also a liminal characteristic named by Turner. Fasting, sleeplessness, and exposure to the elements are part of many rites of passage. Just as Whitman allied himself with the most difficult human circumstances, Dickinson too acknowledges the necessity of pain in the enduring transformation of the threshold:

Essential Oils—are wrung—
The Attar from the Rose
Be not expressed by Suns—alone—
It is the gift of Screws—

The General Rose—decay—
But this—in Lady's Drawer
Make Summer—When the Lady lie
In Ceaseless Rosemary—

Birth and death are at the core of threshold, and death is Dickinson's fascination. She imagines her way into its alabaster chambers, passing its fly-loud, light-failed windows, inquiring again and again what may be found there. Yet those windows also look into an openness and capacity for joy few poets have equaled. Through the seemingly narrow gate of a sequestered life, Dickinson entered a terrain priceless, illimitable—by spreading wide her touchingly described "narrow Hands," she gathered "Paradise."

THERE is one other founding figure of American writing who left an explicit record of taking his place on the threshold: "I went to the woods," wrote Henry David Thoreau, "because I wished to live deliberately, to front only the essential facts of life, and to see if I could not learn what it had to teach, and not, when I came to die, discover that I had not lived." What he wrote in *Walden*'s concluding chapter is worth considering as well:

> I left the woods for as good a reason as I went there. Perhaps it seemed to me that I had several more lives to live, and could not spare any more time for that one. It is remarkable how easily and insensibly we fall into a particular route, and make a beaten track for ourselves. I had not lived there a week before my feet wore a path from my door to the pondside; and though it is five or six years since I trod it, it is still quite distinct. . . . The surface of the earth is soft and impressible by the feet of men; and so with the paths which the mind travels. How worn and dusty, then, must be the highways of the world, how deep the ruts of tradition and conformity! I did not wish to take a cabin passage, but rather to go before the mast and on the deck of the world, for there I could best see the moonlight amid the mountains. I do not wish to go below now.

This second passage clarifies something, and offers a caution: entering the threshold is not a matter of going into the literal woods, though that may help. It is a matter of mind, of leaving the trail of convention and norm, whether in the city or the wild. Naturalist David Lukas has spoken of the danger of surrendering too easily to the names and taxonomies given in field guides: what begins as an aid to seeing and understanding may end by becoming a blindfold, preventing us from seeing other ways the world and its multiple relationships might be named.

A superficial or external marginality can become an identity as conventional as any other, and then it too becomes only a thing to be dropped. Also, the idea of the threshold should not be used to romanticize and so tolerate others' suffering: unchosen homelessness or being forced to the fringes of society by poverty or psychosis are not the same as a liminal life. Despite the lingering social archetype of the "mad artist," madness and artmaking are not the same; where the two coexist, the madness almost always ends up destroying the art, and often the artist as well.

▾   ▾   ▾   ▾   ▾

To speak, and to write, is to assert who we are, what we think. The necessary other side is to surrender these things—to stand humbled and stunned and silent before the wild and inexplicable beauties and mysteries of being. Traditional rites of passage often include a stage of deliberate humbling, when the initiate must accept whatever is said of her without argument. For those who have found themselves in such a position—whether as writers receiving reviews, or as children, spouses, new employees, military recruits, parents, or friends—I offer the good company of the person about to be installed as chief in the Ndembu tribe of Africa. In a ritual Victor Turner calls the "Reviling of the Chief-Elect," the chieftain-to-be is publicly harangued; the purpose is to help him give up his attachment to his former, private way of life and its selfish desires. Each tribal member he has ever slighted reminds him loudly of his failings. He is accused as well of possessing a generally bad character and of greedy actions, and exhorted to give them up:

> You are a mean and selfish fool, one who is bad-tempered! You do not love your fellows, you are only angry with them! Meanness and theft are all you have! . . . Put away meanness, put aside anger, give up adulterous intercouse, give them up immediately! . . . Abstain from witchcraft! . . . You must not be killing people! You must not be ungenerous! . . . You must know the people. . . . If you were mean, and used to eat your cassava mush alone, or your meat alone, today you are in the chieftainship. You must give up your selfish ways . . . you must laugh with everyone . . . you must welcome everyone, you are the chief!

A command traditionally opens this harangue: "Be silent!" The words summon that spacious interval in which the hinge of change may turn. This is the decades-long silence of Komachi as reviled beggar-woman, before her encounter with the priests. It is also the silence that appears in a story about the Buddhist poet, painter, and teacher Hakuin, who wrote in his "Song of Zazen,"

> In this moment, what is there to look for?
> This very place is the Lotus Land.
> This very body is the body of the Buddha.

Just as Komachi is not free of the world of karma, so it was with Hakuin. One day, a girl in the village where he lived became pregnant. Seeking to protect her lover, the son of a neighboring farmer, when her family asked the father's identity she named the young priest. After the child was born, the enraged grandparents brought it to Hakuin's home. "Here," they said, "this is your child, take it!" "Is that so?" Hakuin replied, and reached out his arms.

It was difficult for Hakuin after that—no one is particularly generous with alms to a priest known to have fathered an illegitimate child. But he continued to make his rounds, accepting rice or insults as they came. After a few months, the girl gave in both to her guilt and to her longing for her child. Her parents returned, chastened, to the hut where Hakuin lived. Making profuse apologies, they explained they now knew he was not the father. "Is that so?" Hakuin said, returning the blanketed, well-fed baby to their care.

Freedom from the opinion of others is useful for any who would live in the threshold, and perhaps especially for those who wish to practice art in public; but this story holds another lesson as well. As a person who carries the liminal for his culture, Hakuin's role is to be undefended, to take what is given. Sometimes what is given is rice, sometimes it is derision; sometimes it is a poem or painting, sometimes the call of a scrub jay or backfiring truck engine, sometimes a baby. The heart that knows there is nothing to look for beyond this moment will accept them all. Like the Ndembu chief, it will "laugh with everyone, welcome everyone." Like Komachi, it will be a reed willing to go where the water asks. Whatever wants to enter such a heart will be allowed to enter.

It is the task of the writer to become that permeable and transparent; to become, in the words of Henry James, a person on whom nothing is lost. What is put into the care of such a person will be well tended. Such a person can be trusted to tell the stories she is given to tell, and to tell them with the compassion that comes when the self's deepest interest is not in the self, but in turning outward and into awareness.

I have been trying to sketch here one idea of the creative life, of its means and sources—an idea having to do with the surrender of ordinary conceptions of identity and will for a broader kind of intimacy and allegiance. Ultimately, though, threshold consciousness is not about ideas, whatever they may be. It is, like the act of writing itself, about stepping past what we already think we know and into an entirely new relationship with the many possibilities of being, with the ultimately singular and limitless mystery of being. Above all, it is about freedom, and the affection for all existence that only genuine freedom brings. And so I will close with one more brief poem, written by Gary Snyder, which embraces in its few words and concluding dateline the breadth of threshold life: particular time and timelessness; affection for community in the widest sense; and a person, wandering, returning, making his way—

On Climbing the Sierra Matterhorn
Again After Thirty-One Years

Range after range of mountains
Year after year after year.
I am still in love.

  (4 x 40086, On the summit)

Jane Hirshfield. "Window" by Czeslaw Milosz from *The Collected Poems 1931–1987,* published by Ecco Press; trans. © 1978 by Czeslaw Milosz and Lillian Vallee; reprinted by permission of Czeslaw Milosz. "Gift" by Czeslaw Milosz from *The Collected Poems 1931-1987,* published by Ecco Press, trans. the author, © 1987 Czeslaw Milosz; used by permission of Czeslaw Milosz. "Witchgrass" by Louise Glück from *The Wild Iris,* published by Ecco Press, © 1992 Louise Glück, reprinted by permission of Louise Glück. "The gravid mares" by Virgil from *Eclogues and Georgics of Virgil,* published by Johns Hopkins University Press, trans. © 1990 David Slavitt; used by permission of David Slavitt. "Brother Ivy" by Denise Levertov from *Evening Train,* Copyright © 1992 Denise Levertov; reprinted by permission of New Directions Publishing Corp. "You ask why I make my home in the mountains" by Li Po, from *Banished Immortal,* published by White Pine Press, trans. © 1987 Sam Hamill; reprinted by permission of Sam Hamill. "Poem on the Treasury of the Clear-Seeing Eye" by Eihei Dōgen, trans. © 1991 Jane Hirshfield. "Thirteen Ways of Looking at a Blackbird" by Wallace Stevens from *The Collected Poems,* Copyright © 1923 and renewed 1951 by Wallace Stevens; reprinted by permission of Random House, Inc. "The Choice" by W. B. Yeats, reprinted with the permission of Simon and Schuster from *The Poems of W. B. Yeats: A New Edition,* ed. Richard J. Finneran; © 1933 by Macmillan Publishing Co.; copyright renewed 1961 by Bertha Georgie Yeats. "The Photograph" by Stevie Smith from *Collected Poems of Stevie Smith,* © 1972 Stevie Smith; reprinted by permission of New Directions Publishing Corp. All lines from "The Lion for Real" from *Collected Poems 1947-1980* by Allen Ginsberg, © 1958 by Allen Ginsberg; copyright renewed; reprinted by permission of HarperCollins Publishers, Inc. "The Abnormal is not Courage" from *Monolithos* by Jack Gilbert, Copyright © 1962, 1981 by Jack Gilbert, reprinted by permission of Alfred A. Knopf, Inc. "High Windows" from *Collected Poems,* by Philip Larkin; © 1988, 1989 by the Estate of Philip Larkin; reprinted by permission of Farrar, Straus and Giroux, Inc. "Dolphin" from *Selected Poems* by Robert Lowell; copyright © 1976 by Robert Lowell; reprinted by permission of Farrar, Straus and Giroux, Inc. "Jerome in Solitude" by James Wright from *Above the River: The Complete Poems,* © 1990